Pardhu Thottempudi

Generation and Simulation of Clutter for RADAR Testing Using FPGA

Pardhu Thottempudi

Generation and Simulation of Clutter for RADAR Testing Using FPGA

LAP LAMBERT Academic Publishing

Impressum / Imprint

Bibliografische Information der Deutschen Nationalbibliothek: Die Deutsche Nationalbibliothek verzeichnet diese Publikation in der Deutschen Nationalbibliografie; detaillierte bibliografische Daten sind im Internet über http://dnb.d-nb.de abrufbar.

Alle in diesem Buch genannten Marken und Produktnamen unterliegen warenzeichen-, marken- oder patentrechtlichem Schutz bzw. sind Warenzeichen oder eingetragene Warenzeichen der jeweiligen Inhaber. Die Wiedergabe von Marken, Produktnamen, Gebrauchsnamen, Handelsnamen, Warenbezeichnungen u.s.w. in diesem Werk berechtigt auch ohne besondere Kennzeichnung nicht zu der Annahme, dass solche Namen im Sinne der Warenzeichen- und Markenschutzgesetzgebung als frei zu betrachten wären und daher von jedermann benutzt werden dürften.

Bibliographic information published by the Deutsche Nationalbibliothek: The Deutsche Nationalbibliothek lists this publication in the Deutsche Nationalbibliografie; detailed bibliographic data are available in the Internet at http://dnb.d-nb.de.

Any brand names and product names mentioned in this book are subject to trademark, brand or patent protection and are trademarks or registered trademarks of their respective holders. The use of brand names, product names, common names, trade names, product descriptions etc. even without a particular marking in this work is in no way to be construed to mean that such names may be regarded as unrestricted in respect of trademark and brand protection legislation and could thus be used by anyone.

Coverbild / Cover image: www.ingimage.com

Verlag / Publisher:
LAP LAMBERT Academic Publishing
ist ein Imprint der / is a trademark of
OmniScriptum GmbH & Co. KG
Heinrich-Böcking-Str. 6-8, 66121 Saarbrücken, Deutschland / Germany
Email: info@lap-publishing.com

Herstellung: siehe letzte Seite /
Printed at: see last page
ISBN: 978-3-659-75129-5

 **Pardhu Thottempudi** became a Member (M) of IEEE in 2015. Pardhu was born in Luxettipet village in Adilabad district in Telangana state, India. He completed Batchelor's Degree B.tech in the stream of Electronics and Communication Engineering in 2011 from MLR Institute of Technology, Hyderabad, India. He has done his Master's Degree M.Tech in Embedded Systems from Vignan's University, Vadlamudi in 2013. His major fields of interests include Digital signal processing, RADAR communications, Embedded systems, implementation of signal processing on applicationsin FPGA.

He is working as Assistant Professor of Department of Electronics and Communication Engineering in Marri Laxman Reddy Institute of Technology & management, Hyderabad, India since 2014. Previously he worked as Assistant professor in Brilliant Group of Technical Institutions, Hyderabad, India. He also worked as project intern in Research Centre Imarat, Hyderabad. He published 18 research papers on VLSI, Image Processing, Antennas, Signal processing, RADAR Communications in Reputed International Journals and Various IEEE Conferences.

Pardhu Thottempudi is the Life member of ISTE, Associate Member of IETE from 2015. He filed a patent on "Power Efficient Compressor Using Full Adder Circuit". He is the member of IEEE signal Processing society, IEEE Industrial Electronics Society.

ACKNOWLEDGEMENT

With great pleasure I want to take this opportunity to express our heartfelt gratitude to all the people who helped in making this project a grand success.

I am glad to express my intense pleasure and thanks to **Dr. C.G. Balaji**, Scientist 'H', RCI, DRDO for giving us an opportunity to undergo this project and **Mr. P. Suresh**, Scientist 'C' and **Mr.Someshwara Rao**, Scientist 'E' for their tremendous and immense guidance and insight discussions during the project which made my task easier to complete the project successfully.

I express my heartfelt thanks to **Mrs. N. Usha Rani**, Associate Professor, School of Electronics, Vignan University, for her valuable guidance, and encouragement during my project.

I wish to express my deep sense of gratitude to **Mr. K. Vijaya Kumar** sir, Associate Professor and Project coordinator for his able guidance and useful suggestions, which helped me in completing the project work, in time.

I also express my heartfelt thanks to, **Dr. B. SeethaRamanjaneyulu,** Professor and Head of the Department of School of Electronics, Vignan University, for his intense support and encouragement during my project.

I show gratitude to our honourable Principal **Dr. V. Madhusudhana Rao** for having provided all the facilities and support. I also thank all the teaching and non-teaching staff of our School of Electronics for their valuable support and generous advice.

I express my heartfelt thanks to **Mr. M. Rambabu** , STA ,**Mr. B. Veerendra**, SC'C and technical staff who supported my work at RCI.

Finally thanks to our parents and friends for their continuous support and enthusiastic help.

T.PARDHU

CONTENTS

LIST OF FIGURES

LIST OF TABLES

CHAPTER 1

INTRODUCTION

1.1 Over View:

Clutter is a term used to describe any object that may generate unwanted radar returns that may interfere with normal radar operations. Parasitic returns that enter the radar through the antenna's main lobe are called main lobe clutter; otherwise they are called side lobe clutter. Clutter can be classified in two main categories: surface clutter and airborne or volume clutter. Surface clutter includes trees, vegetation, ground terrain, man-made structures, and sea surface (sea clutter). Volume clutter normally has large extent (size) and includes chaff, rain, birds, and insects. Chaff consists of a large number of small dipole reflectors that have large RCS values. It is released by hostile aircaft or missiles as a means of ECM in an attempt to confuse the defense. Surface clutter changes from one area to another, while volume clutter may be more predictable.

1.2 Motivation:

Radars are used mainly for all Defence purposes, and Clutter is a property of Radar. The determination and verification of different targets in a regular Radar system can be avoided using Simulators. It is cost effective and less time consuming and can be done. Radar Target Echo simulators form an essential requirement in the defence industry for electronic countermeasure and performance evaluation of radars.[1]

1.3 History:

Radar is an object detection system which uses radio waves to determine the range, altitude, direction, or speed of objects. As early as 1886, German physicist Heinrich Hertz showed that radio waves could be reflected from solid objects. In 1905 the German inventor Christian Hülsmeyer was the first to use radio waves to detect "the presence of distant

1

metallic objects". It can be used to detect aircraft, ships, spacecraft, guided missiles, motor vehicles, weather formations, and terrain. Radar was secretly developed by several nations before and during World War II. The term RADAR was coined in 1940 by the United States Navy as an acronym for Radio Detection And Ranging. The modern uses of radar are highly diverse, including air traffic control, radar astronomy, air-defence systems, antimissile systems; marine radars to locate landmarks and other ships; aircraft anti-collision systems; ocean surveillance systems, outer space surveillance and rendezvous systems; meteorological precipitation monitoring; altimetry and flight control systems; guided missile target locating systems; and ground-penetrating radar for geological observations. High tech radar systems are associated with digital signal processing and are capable of extracting useful information from very high noise levels.

1.4 Organization of thesis:

This complete book describes about the whole project. This Report is divided into several chapters; Chapter1 discusses about overview of project, statement of problem, motivation, history, literature survey, organization of thesis, Chapter 2 completely discuss about Radars basics , Chapter 3 describes about clutter and types of clutter and equations of different clutters, Chapter 4 is about the Description of Softwares and hardwares used, Chapter 5 is about the Experimental work, Chapter 6 is about Project working and Results, Chapter 7 is about Future scope and conclusion.

CHAPTER 2

RADAR BASICS

Radar is a system that uses electromagnetic waves to identify the range, altitude, direction, or speed of both moving and fixed objects such as aircraft, ships, motor vehicles, weather formations, and terrain. The term RADAR was coined in 1941 as an acronym for Radio Detection and Ranging.

2.1 PRINCIPLE OF RADARS:

A radar system has a transmitter that emits radio waves called radar signals in predetermined directions. When these come into contact with an object they are usually reflected or scattered in many directions. Radar signals are reflected especially well by materials of considerable electrical conductivity especially by most metals, by seawater and by wet lands. The radar signals that are reflected back towards the transmitter are the desirable ones that make radar work. If the object is moving either toward or away from the transmitter, there is a slight equivalent change in the frequency of the radio waves, caused by the Doppler Effect. This change in frequency is used to detect the velocity of target.[1]

Radar receivers are usually, but not always, in the same location as the transmitter. Although the reflected radar signals captured by the receiving antenna are usually very weak, they can be strengthened by electronic amplifiers. The weak absorption of radio waves by the medium through which it passes is what enables radar sets to detect objects at relatively long ranges, ranges at which other electromagnetic wavelengths, such as visible light, infrared light, and ultraviolet light, are too strongly attenuated. The process of directing artificial radio waves towards objects is called illumination. If electromagnetic waves travelling through one material meet another, having a very different dielectric constant or diamagnetic constant from the first, the waves will reflect or scatter from the boundary between the materials. This means that a solid object in air or in a vacuum, or a significant change in atomic density between the object and

3

what is surrounding it, will usually scatter radar (radio) waves from its surface. Radar waves scatter in a variety of ways depending on the size (wavelength) of the radio wave and the shape of the target. If the wavelength is much shorter than the target's size, the wave will bounce off in a way similar to the way light is reflected by a mirror. If the wavelength is much longer than the size of the target, the target may not be visible because of poor reflection.

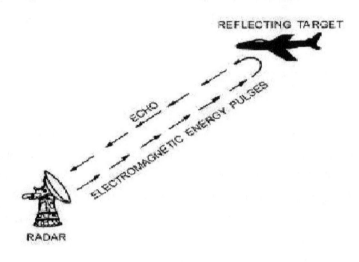

Figure 2.1: Principle of RADAR

4

2.2 RADAR Equation:

The radar equation is used to predict the echo power received by the receiving antenna. The amount of power P_r returning to receiving antenna is given by the following equation.

$$P_r = \frac{P_t.G_t.A_r.\sigma.F^4}{(4\pi)^2.R_t^2.R_r^2}$$

Where

- P_t = transmitter power
- G_t = gain of the transmitting antenna
- A_r = effective aperture (area) of the receiving antenna
- σ = radar cross section of the target
- F = pattern propagation factor
- R_t = distance from the transmitter to the target
- R_r = distance from the target to the receiver.

2.3 Testing of RADAR systems:

Radar target simulators form an essential requirement in the defence industry for electronic countermeasure and performance evaluation of radars. A radar target simulator simulates the received echo power, which is used for testing of radar. For simulating the received power the parameters in the radar equation need to be simulated. In this project we simulate and generate Clutter signal using Field Programmable Gate Array (FPGA) and LABveiw(NI).

CHAPTER 3

CLUTTER

3.1. Clutter Definition:

Clutter is a term used to describe any object that may generate unwanted radar returns that may interfere with normal radar operations. Parasitic returns that enter the radar through the antenna's main lobe are called main lobe clutter; otherwise they are called side lobe clutter. Clutter can be classified in two main categories: surface clutter and airborne or volume clutter. Surface clutter includes trees, vegetation, ground terrain, man-made structures, and sea surface (sea clutter). Volume clutter normally has large extent (size) and includes chaff, rain, birds, and insects. Chaff consists of a large number of small dipole reflectors that have large RCS values. It is released by hostile aircaft or missiles as a means of ECM in an attempt to confuse the defense. Surface clutter changes from one area to another, while volume clutter may be more predictable.[3]

Clutter echoes are random and have thermal noise-like characteristics because the individual clutter components (scatterers) have random phases and amplitudes. In many cases, the clutter signal level is much higher than the receiver noise level. Thus, the radar's ability to detect targets embedded in high clutter background depends on the Signal-to-Clutter Ratio (SCR) rather than the SNR.

White noise normally introduces the same amount of noise power across all radar range bins, while clutter power may vary within a single range bin. And since clutter returns are target-like echoes, the only way a radar can distinguish target returns from clutter echoes is based on the target RCS σt , and the anticipated clutter RCS σc (via clutter map). Clutter RCS can be defined as the equivalent radar cross section attributed to reflections from a clutter area, Ac .The average clutter RCS is given by

$$\sigma_c = \sigma^0 A_c$$ ....(3.1)

where $\sigma^0 (m^2/m^2)$ is the clutter scattering coefficient, a dimensionless quantity that is often expressed in dB. Some radar engineers express σ^0 in terms of squared centimeters per squared meter. In these cases, σ^0 is $40dB$ higher than normal.

The term that describes the constructive/destructive interference of the electromagnetic waves diffracted from an object (target or clutter) is called the propagation factor .Since target and clutter returns have different angles of arrival (different propagation factors), we can define the SCR as

$$ SCR = \frac{\sigma_t F_t^2 F_r^2}{\sigma_c F_c^2} $$

....(3.2)

where F_c is the clutter propagation factor, F_t and F_r are, respectively, the transmit and receive propagation factors for the target. In many cases

$F_t = F_r$.

3.2. Surface Clutter:

Surface clutter includes both land and sea clutter, and is often called area clutter. Area clutter manifests itself in airborne radars in the look-down mode.It is also a major concern for ground-based radars when searching for targets at low grazing angles. The grazing angle ψg is the angle from the surface of the earth to the main axis of the illuminating beam, as illustrated in Fig. 3.1.

Figure 3.1: Definition of grazing angle

Three factors affect the amount of clutter in the radar beam. They are the grazing angle, surface roughness, and the radar wavelength. Typically, the clutter scattering coefficient σ0 is larger for smaller wavelengths. Fig.2 shows a sketch describing the dependency of σ0 on the grazing angle. Three regions are identified; they are the low grazing angle region, flat or plateau region, and the high grazing angle region.

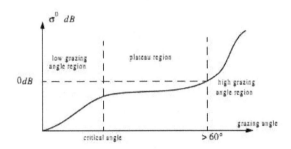

Figure 3.2 : Clutter Regions

The low grazing angle region extends from zero to about the critical angle. The critical angle is defined by Rayleigh as the angle below which a surface is considered to be smooth, and above which a surface is considered to be rough.Denote the root mean square (rms) of a surface height irregularity as h_{rms} , then according to the Rayleigh critera the surface is considered to be smooth if

$$\frac{4\pi h_{rms}}{\lambda}\sin\psi_g < \frac{\pi}{2}$$

....(3.3)

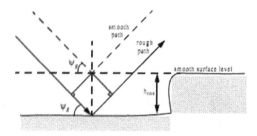

Figure 3.3: Rough surface definition

Consider a wave incident on a rough surface, as shown in Fig. 3.3. Due to surface height irregularity (surface roughness), the "rough path" is longer than the "smooth path" by a distance $2h_{rms}\sin\psi_g$. This path difference translates into a phase differential $\Delta\psi$:

$$\Delta\psi = \frac{2\pi}{\lambda} \, 2h_{rms}\sin\psi_g$$

..................................(3.4)

The critical angle ψ_{gc} is then computed when $\Delta\psi = \pi$ (first null), thus

$$\frac{4\pi h_{rms}}{\lambda} \sin\psi_{gc} = \pi$$

..................................(3.5)

Or equivalently,

$$\psi_{gc} = a\sin\frac{\lambda}{4h_{rms}}$$

..................................(3.6)

In the case of sea clutter, for example, the rms surface height irregularity is

$$h_{rms} = 0.025 + 0.046 \, S_{state}^{1.72}$$

..................................(3.7)

9

where S_{state} is the sea state. The sea state is characterized by the wave height, period, length, particle velocity,and wind velocity. For example, $S_{state} = 3$ refers to a moderate sea state,where in this case the wave height is approximately equal to between 0.9144 to 1.2192 m, the wave period 3.5 to 4.5 seconds, wave length 1.9812 to 33.528 m , wave velocity 20.372 to 25.928 Km/hr , and windvelocity 22.224 to 29.632 Km/hr .

Clutter at low grazing angles is often referred to as diffused clutter, where there are a large number of clutter returns in the radar beam (non-coherent reflections). In the flat region the dependency of σ^0 on the grazing angle is minimal. Clutter in the high grazing angle region is more specular (coherent reflections) and the diffuse clutter components disappear. In this region the smooth surfaces have larger σ^0 than rough surfaces, opposite of the low grazing angle region.

3.2.1. Radar Equation for Area Clutter:

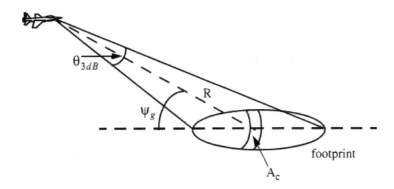

Figure 3.4 : Airborne radar in the look-down mode

Consider an airborne radar in the look-down mode shown in Fig. 3.4. The intersection of the antenna beam with ground defines an elliptically shaped footprint. The size of the footprint is a function of the grazing angle and the antenna 3dB beam width θ_{3dB} , as illustrated in

10

Fig. 3.5. The footprint is divided into many ground range bins each of size $(c\tau/2)\sec\psi_g$, where τ is the pulse width.

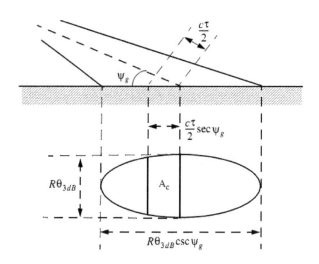

Figure 3.5: Footprint Definition

From Fig. 3.5, the clutter area A_c is

$$A_c \approx R\theta_{3dB} \frac{c\tau}{2} \sec\psi_g$$

$$\dots\dots\dots\dots\dots\dots\dots\dots\dots(3.8)$$

The power received by the radar from a scatterer within A_c is given by the radar equation as

$$S_t = \frac{P_t G^2 \lambda^2 \sigma_t}{(4\pi)^3 R^4}$$

$$\dots\dots\dots\dots\dots\dots\dots\dots\dots\dots(3.9)$$

11

where as usual, P_t is the peak transmitted power, G is the antenna gain, λ is the wavelength, σ_t and is the target RCS. Similarly, the received power from clutter is

$$S_{Ac} = \frac{P_t G^2 \lambda^2 \sigma_c}{(4\pi)^3 R^4}$$

$$\dotfill (3.10)$$

where the subscript A_c is used for area clutter. Substituting Eq. (3.1) for σ_c into Eq. (3.10), we can then obtain the SCR for area clutter by dividing Eq.(3.9) by Eq. (3.10). More precisely,

$$(SCR)_{Ac} = \frac{2\sigma_t \cos\psi_g}{\sigma^0 \theta_{3dB} R c \tau}$$

$$\dotfill (3.11)$$

3.3. Volume Clutter:

Volume clutter has large extents and includes rain (weather), chaff, birds,and insects. The volume clutter coefficient is normally expressed in squared meters (RCS per resolution volume). Birds, insects, and other flying particles are often referred to as angel clutter or biological clutter. The average RCS for individual birds or insects as a function of the weight of the bird or insect is

$$(\sigma_b)_{dBsm} \approx -46 + 5.8\log W_b$$

$$\dotfill (3.12)$$

where W_b is the individual bird or insect weight in grams. Bird and insect RCSs are also a function of frequency; for example, a pigeon's average RCS is $-26dBsm$ at S-band, and is equal to $-27dBsm$ at X-band.

As mentioned earlier, chaff is used as an ECM technique by hostile forces. It consists of a large number of dipole reflectors with large RCS values. Historically, chaff was made of aluminum foil; however, in recent years most chaff is made of the more rigid fiber glass with conductive coating. The maximum chaff RCS occurs when the dipole length L is one half the radar wavelength. The average RCS for a single dipole when viewed broadside is

$$\sigma_{chaff1} \approx 0.88\lambda^2 \quad\quad\quad ....(3.13)$$

and for an average aspect angle, it drops to

$$\sigma_{chaff1} \approx 0.15\lambda^2 \quad\quad\quad ....(3.14)$$

where the subscript $chaff1$ is used to indicate a single dipole, and λ is the radar wavelength. The total chaff RCS within a radar resolution volume is

$$\sigma_{chaff} \approx 0.15\lambda^2 N_D \quad\quad\quad ....(3.15)$$

where N_D is the total number of dipoles in the resolution volume.

Weather or rain clutter is easier to suppress than chaff, since rain droplets can be viewed as perfect small spheres. We can use the Rayleigh approxima-tion of perfect sphere to estimate the rain droplets' RCS. The Rayleigh approx-imation, without regard to the propagation medium index of refraction, is given in Eq. (3.16)

$$\sigma = 9\pi r^2 (kr)^4 \quad\quad r \ll \lambda \quad\quad ....(3.16)$$

Where $k = 2\pi/\lambda$, and r is radius of a rain droplet.

Electromagnetic waves when reflected from a perfect sphere become strongly co-polarized (have the same polarization as the incident waves). Consequently, if the radar transmits, say, a right-hand-circularly (RHC) polarized wave, then the received waves are left-hand-circularly (LHC) polarized, because it is propagating in the opposite direction. Therefore, the back-scattered energy from rain droplets retains the same wave rotation (polarization) as the incident wave, but has a reversed direction of propagation. It follows that radars can suppress rain clutter by co-polarizing the radar transmit and receive antennas.

13

Defining η as RCS per unit resolution volume V_W, it is computed as the sum of all individual scatterers RCS within the volume,

$$\eta = \sum_{i=1}^{N} \sigma_i$$

....(3.17)

where N is the total number of scatterers within the resolution volume. Thus, the total RCS of a single resolution volume is

$$\sigma_W = \sum_{i=1}^{N} \sigma_i V_W$$

....(3.18)

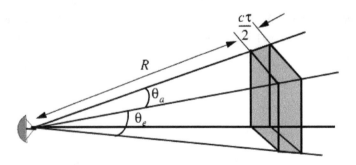

Figure 3.6 : Definition of a Resolution Volume

A resolution volume is shown in Fig. 3.6, and is approximated by

$$V_W \approx \frac{\pi}{8} \theta_a \theta_e R^2 c \tau$$

....(3.19)

where θ_a, θ_e are, respectively, the antenna beam width in azimuth and elevation, τ is the pulse width in seconds, c is speed of light, and R is range.

Consider a propagation medium with an index of refraction m. The ith rain droplet RCS approximation in this medium is

$$\sigma_i \approx \frac{\pi^5}{\lambda^4} K^2 D_i^6$$

....(3.20)

Where

$$K^2 = \left| \frac{m^2 - 1}{m^2 + 2} \right|^2$$

....(3.21)

and D_i is the ith droplet diameter. For example, temperatures between $32°F$ and yield $68°F$

$$\sigma_i \approx 0.93 \frac{\pi^5}{\lambda^4} D_i^6$$

....(3.22)

and for ice Eq. (3.20) can be approximated by

$$\sigma_i \approx 0.2 \frac{\pi^5}{\lambda^4} D_i^6$$

....(3.23)

Substituting Eq. (3.20) into Eq. (3.17) yields

$$\eta = \frac{\pi^5}{\lambda^4} K^2 Z$$

....(3.24)

15

where the weather clutter coefficient Z is defined as

$$Z = \sum_{i=1}^{N} D_i^6$$

....(3.25)

In general, a rain droplet diameter is given in millimeters and the radar resolution volume in expressed in cubic meters, thus the units of Z are often expressed in $milliemeter^6/m^3$.

3.3.1. Radar Equation for Volume Clutter:

The radar equation gives the total power received by the radar from a σ_t target at range R as

$$S_t = \frac{P_t G^2 \lambda^2 \sigma_t}{(4\pi)^3 R^4}$$

....(3.26)

where all parameters in Eq. (3.26) have been defined earlier. The weather clutter power received by the radar is

$$S_W = \frac{P_t G^2 \lambda^2 \sigma_W}{(4\pi)^3 R^4}$$

....(3.27)

Using Eq. (3.18) and Eq. (3.19) into Eq. (3.27) and collecting terms yield

$$S_W = \frac{P_t G^2 \lambda^2}{(4\pi)^3 R^4} \frac{\pi}{8} R^2 \theta_a \theta_e c\tau \sum_{i=1}^{N} \sigma_i$$

...........................(3.28)

16

The SCR for weather clutter is then computed by dividing Eq. (3.26) by Eq.(3.28). More precisely,

$$(SCR)_V = \frac{S_t}{S_W} = \frac{8\sigma_t}{\pi\theta_a\theta_e c\tau R^2 \sum\limits_{i=1}^{N} \sigma_i}$$

...............................(3.29)

where the subscript V is used to denote volume clutter.

3.4. Clutter Statistical Models:

Since clutter within a resolution cell (or volume) is composed of a large number of scatterers with random phases and amplitudes, it is statistically described by a probability distribution function. The type of distribution depends on the nature of clutter itself (sea, land, volume), the radar operating frequency, and the grazing angle.

If sea or land clutter is composed of many small scatterers when the probability of receiving an echo from one scatterer is statistically independent of the echo received from another scatterer, then the clutter may be modeled using a Rayleigh distribution,

$$f(x) = \frac{2x}{x_0}\exp\left(\frac{-x^2}{x_0}\right) \; ; \; x \geq 0$$

...........................(3.30)

Where x_0 is the mean squared value of x.

The log-normal distribution best describes land clutter at low grazing angles. It also fits sea clutter in the plateau region. It is given by

17

$$f(x) = \frac{1}{\sigma\sqrt{2\pi}\,x} \exp\left(-\frac{(\ln x - \ln x_m)^2}{2\sigma^2}\right) \; ; \; x > 0$$

............(3.31)

Where x_m is the median of the random variable x , and σ is the standard deviation of the random variable $\ln(x)$.

The Weibull distribution is used to model clutter at low grazing angles (less than five degrees) for frequencies between 1 and $10 GHz$. The Weibull probability density function is determined by the Weibull slope parameter (often tabulated) and a median scatter coefficient $\overline{\sigma}_0$, and is given by

$$f(x) = \frac{bx^{b-1}}{\overline{\sigma}_0} \exp\left(-\frac{x^b}{\overline{\sigma}_0}\right) \; ; \; x \geq 0$$

.....................(3.32)

where $b = 1/a$ is known as the shape parameter. Note that when $b = 2$ the Weibull distribution becomes a Rayleigh distribution.

3.5. Clutter Spectrum:

The power spectrum of stationary clutter (zero Doppler) can be represented by a delta function. However, clutter is not always stationary; it actually exhibits some Doppler frequency spread because of wind speed and motion of the radar scanning antenna. In general, the clutter spectrum is concentrated around $f = 0$ and integer multiples of the radar PRF f_r , and may exhibit some small spreading.

The clutter power spectrum can be written as the sum of fixed (stationary) and random (due to frequency spreading) components. For most cases, the random component is Gaussian. If we denote the fixed to the random power ratio by W^2, then we can write the clutter spectrum as

$$S_c(\omega) = \bar{\sigma}_0 \left(\frac{W^2}{1 + W^2} \right) \delta(\omega_0) + \frac{\bar{\sigma}_0}{(1 + W^2)\sqrt{2\pi\sigma_\omega^2}} \exp\left(-\frac{(\omega - \omega_0)^2}{2\sigma_\omega^2} \right)$$
(3.33)

Where $\omega_0 = 2\pi f_0$ is the radar operating frequency in radians per second, σ_ω is the rms frequency spread component (determines the Doppler frequency spread), and $\bar{\sigma}_0$ is the Weibull parameter.

The first term of the right-hand side of Eq. (3.33) represents the PSD for stationary clutter, while the second term accounts for the frequency spreading.Nevertheless, since most of the clutter power is concentrated around zero Doppler with some spreading (typically less than 100 Hz), it is customary to model clutter using a Gaussian-shaped power spectrum (which is easier to analyze than Eq. (3.33)). More precisely,

$$S_c(\omega) = \frac{P_c}{\sqrt{2\pi\sigma_\omega^2}} \exp\left(-\frac{(\omega - \omega_0)^2}{2\sigma_\omega^2} \right)$$
.....................(3.34)

where P_c is the total clutter power; σ_ω^2 and ω_0 were defined earlier.

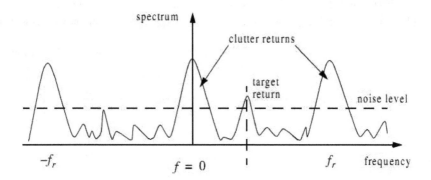

Figure.3.7: Typical radar return PSD when clutter and target are present

Fig. 3.7 shows a typical PSD sketch of radar returns when both target and clutter are present. Note that the clutter power is concentrated around DC and integer multiples of the PRF.

CHAPTER 4

HARDWARE AND SOFTWARE DESCRIPTION

4.1 MATLAB:

The name MATLAB stands for MATrix LABoratory. MATLAB was written originally to provide easy access to matrix software developed by the LINPACK (linear system package) and EISPACK (Eigen system package) projects.

MATLAB is a high-performance language for technical computing. It integrates computation, visualization, and programming environment. Furthermore, MATLAB is a modern programming language environment. It has sophisticated data structures, contains built-in editing and debugging tools, and supports object-oriented programming. These factors make MATLAB an excellent tool for teaching and research.MATLAB has many advantages compared to conventional computer languages for solving technical problems.

MATLAB is an interactive system whose basic data element is an array that does not require dimensioning.It has powerful built-in routines that enable a very wide variety of computations. It also has easy to use graphics commands that make the visualization of results immediately available. Special applications are collected in packages referred to as toolbox. There are toolboxes for signal processing, symbolic computation, control theory, simulation, optimization, and several other fields of applied science and engineering.[7]

MATLAB R2012a is used in the project for simulation of the Radar Cross Section.

4.1.1 MATLAB Workspace:

MATLAB workspace is as shown in figure 4.1.

Figure 4.1: Graphical interface to MATLAB Workspace

4.1.2 M-file Scripts in MATLAB:

A script file is an external file that contains a sequence of MATLAB statements. Script files have a filename extension '.m' and are often called M-files. M-files can be scripts that simply execute a series of MATLAB statements, or they can be functions that can accept arguments and can produce one or more outputs.

For creating a new file select File → New → Script or Click the new file button on the toolbar or Press ctrl + N. **Figure 4.2** shows how to create a new M-file.

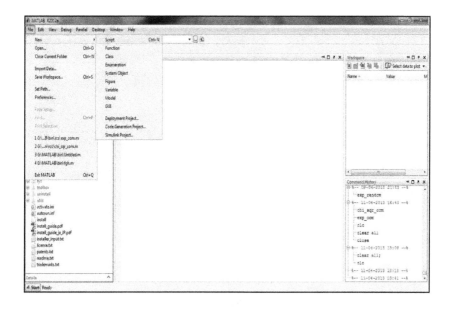

Figure 4.2: Creating new M-file in MATLAB

A new editor window opens for creating the M-file. To run the script select debug → run 'filename.m' in the editor window or click run button on toolbar or press F5. Figure 4.3 shows running a script.[6]

Figure 4.3: executing a script in MATLAB

4.2 Xilinx ISE:

The Xilinx ISE is a complete FPGA programmable logic design suite providing:

- Specification of programmable logic via schematic capture or Verilog/VHDL
- Synthesis and Place & Route of specified logic for various Xilinx FPGAs and CPLDs
- Functional (Behavioural) and Timing (post-Place & Route) simulation
- Download of configuration data into target device via communications cable

Xilinx ISE 12.1 is used in this project for simulating and for configuration of FPGA.

4.2.1 Creating a Project with Xilinx ISE:

To create a new project first, open the project navigator. To start the Xilinx Project Navigator, click on the Start menu and select All Programs → Xilinx ISE Design Suite 12.1 → ISE Design Tools → 32bit Project Navigator.

To create a new project for the design select: File → New Project. A window as shown in **Figure 4.4** opens.

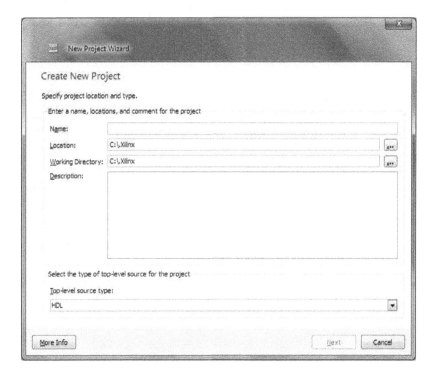

Figure 4.4: New Project Wizard in Xilinx Project Navigator

Enter the details in the window.

1. Name: Enter a project name.
2. Location: Select a project location. Any directories will be built automatically.
3. Select HDL for the "Top-Level Source Type:"
4. Click Next.

A window for entering the details of targeted FPGA appears. This window is as shown in **Figure 4.5.**

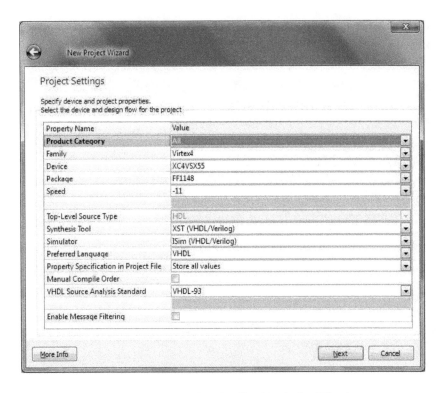

Figure 4.5: Project Settings in Xilinx New Project Wizard

Enter the details such a FPGA family, device, package, synthesis tool, etc for the project. Click Next. A window as shown in **Figure 4.6** is displaying the summary of details entered appears. Check the details and click Finish.

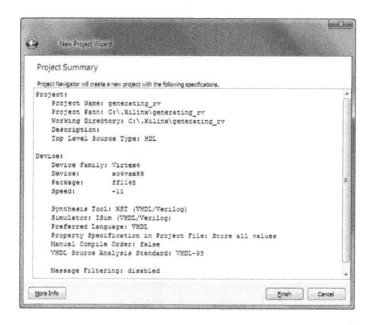

Figure 4.6: Project summary in New Project Wizard

The ISE Project Navigator window will now be active. This is shown in **Figure 4.7.**

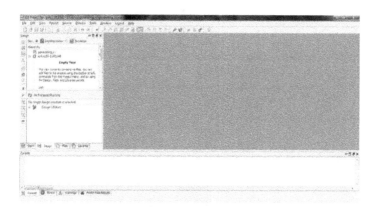

Figure 4.7: Xilinx Project Navigator

To add a new source to project select Project → New source or right click in the hierarchy view in design panel and select new source. A new source wizard window as in **Figure 4.8** appears. Select the required source and enter the details. Add the required sources such as VHDL module, IP Core etc.

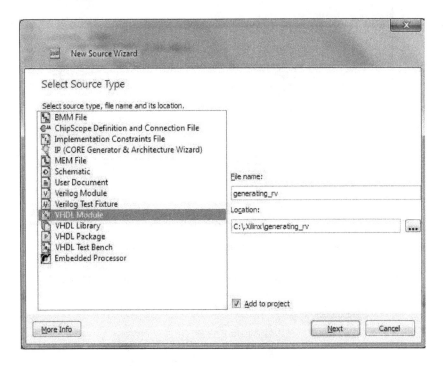

Figure 4.8: Adding New source to Xilinx Project Navigator

4.2.2 Simulation of a Project:

For simulating the design from the Project Navigator:

1. In the Design Panel, select the Simulation view
2. From the drop down menu below the Simulation radial button, select Behavioural.
3. In the project Hierarchy pane select VHDL file.

4. In the Processes frame, double click Simulate Behavioural Model or click the Play button.

This will launch the ModelSim simulator to simulate the design. This simulator window is as shown in **Figure 4.9** opens. In the simulator window values for different signal can be assigned and simulated.

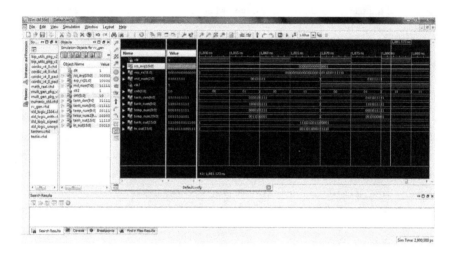

Figure 4.9: Simulation of a Project in Xilinx Project Navigator

4.2.3 Implementation of a Project using Chip-scope Pro:

Chip-Scope Pro tool inserts logic analyser, system analyser, and virtual I/O low-profile software cores directly into your design, allowing you to view any internal signal or node, including embedded hard or soft processors. Signals are captured in the system at the speed of operation and brought out through the programming interface, freeing up pins for your design. Captured signals are then displayed and analysed using the Chip-Scope Pro Analyser tool.

The Chip Scope Pro tool also interfaces with your Agilent Technologies bench test equipment through the ATC2 software core. This core synchronizes the ChipScope Pro tool to Agilent's FPGA Dynamic Probe add-on option. This unique partnership between Xilinx and

Agilent gives you deeper trace memory, faster clock speeds, more trigger options, and system-level measurement capability all while using fewer pins on the FPGA device.

The ChipScope Pro Serial I/O Toolkit provides a fast, easy, and interactive setup and debug of serial I/O channels in high-speed FPGA designs. The ChipScope Pro Serial I/O Toolkit allows you to take bit-error ratio (BER) measurements on multiple channels and adjust high-speed serial transceiver parameters in real-time while your serial I/O channels interact with the rest of the system.[7]

4.2.4: VHDL:

VHDL (VHSIC Hardware Description Language) is a hardware description language used in electronic design automation to describe digital and mixed-signal systems such as field-programmable gate array sand integrated circuits. VHDL can also be used as a general purpose parallel programming language. VHDL usage has risen rapidly since its inception andis used by literally tens of thousands of engineers aroundthe globe to create sophisticated electronic products.VHDL is a powerful languagewith numerous language constructs that are capable ofdescribing very complex behaviour.

The advantages of VHDL are:

• VHDL supports unsynthesizable constructs that are useful in writing high-level models, testbenches and other non-hardware or non-synthesizable artefact's that we need in hardware design.
• VHDL can be used throughout a large portion of the design process in different capacities, from specification to implementation to verification.
• VHDL has static type checking, many errors can be caught before synthesis and/or simulation.
• VHDL has a rich collection of datatypes
• VHDL is a full-featured language with a good module system (libraries and packages).
• VHDL has a well-defined standard.

Some basic terms in VHDL are:

Entity: All designs are expressed in terms of entities. An entity isthe most basic building block in a design. The uppermost level ofthe design is the top-level entity. If the design is hierarchical, thenthe top-level description will have lower-level descriptions contained in it. These lower-level descriptions will be lower-level entitiescontained in the top-level entity description.

Architecture: All entities that can be simulated have an architecturedescription. The architecture describes the behaviour of theentity. A single entity can have multiple architectures. One architecture might be behavioural while another might be a structuraldescription of the design.

Configuration:A configuration statement is used to bind a component instance to an entity-architecture pair. A configuration can be considered like a parts list for a design. It describes whichbehaviour to use for each entity, much like a parts list describeswhich part to use for each part in the design.

Package:A package is a collection of commonly used data typesand subprograms used in a design. Think of a package as a toolboxthat contains tools used to build designs.

Driver: This is a source on a signal. If a signal is driven by twosources, then when both sources are active, the signal will havetwo drivers.

Bus: The term "bus" usually brings to mind a group of signals ora particular method of communication used in the design of hardware.In VHDL, a bus is a special kind of signal that may have itsdrivers turned off.

Attribute: An attribute is data that are attached to VHDL objectsor predefined data about VHDL objects. Examples are the currentdrive capability of a buffer or the maximum operating temperatureof the device.

Generic:A generic is VHDL's term for a parameter that passesinformation to an entity. For instance, if an entity is a gate levelmodel with a rise and a fall delay, values for the rise and fall delayscould be passed into the entity with generics.

Process:A process is the basic unit of execution in VHDL. All operations that are performed in a simulation of a VHDL descriptionare broken into single or multiple processes

4.2.5: Intellectual Property Core (IPcore):

In electronic design a semiconductor intellectual property core, IP core, or IP block is a reusable unit of logic, cell, or chip layout design that is the intellectual of one party. IP cores may be licensed to another party or can be owned and used by a single party alone. The term is derived from the licensing of the patent and/or source code copyright that exist in the design. IP cores can be used as building blocks within ASIC chip designs or FPGA logic designs. IP cores in the electronic design industry have had a profound impact on the design of systems on a chip. By licensing a design multiple times, an IP core licensor spreads the cost of development among multiple chip makers. IP cores for standard processors, interfaces, and internal functions have enabled chip makers to put more of their resources into developing the differentiating features of their chips. As a result, chip makers have developed innovations more quickly.

Intellectual Property (IP) are key building blocks of Xilinx Targeted Design Platforms. Xilinx FPGA devices and tools are architected for easy creation of Plug-and-Play IP; allowing Xilinx and its Alliance Program Members to provide an extensive catalog of cores to address your general and market specific needs. This enables you to focus your design efforts on where you differentiate your product from your competition and accelerate your time to profit.

CORDIC 4.0 IPcore is used in this project to calculate the arctanh, cosine, square-root of a number.

4.2.5.1: CORDIC IPcore:

CORDIC (**CO**ordinate **R**otation **DI**gital Computer), also known as the digit-by-digit method and Volder's algorithm, is a simple and efficient algorithm to do the calculate hyperbolic and trigonometric functions. It is commonly used when no hardware multiplier is available (e.g., simple microcontrollers and FPGAs) as the only operations it requires are addition, subtraction, bitshift and table lookup.

The modern CORDIC algorithm was first described in 1959 by Jack E. Volder. It was developed at the aero electronics department of Convair to replace the analog resolver in the B 58 bomber's navigation computer.Although CORDIC is similar to mathematical techniques published by Henry Briggs as early as 1624, it is optimized for low complexity finite state CPUs. John Stephen Walther at Hewlett-Packard further generalized the algorithm, allowing it to calculate hyperbolic and exponential functions, logarithms, multiplications, divisions, and square roots. Originally, CORDIC was implemented using the binary numeral system. In the 1970s, decimal CORDIC became widely used in pocket calculators, most of which operate in binary-coded-decimal (BCD) rather than binary. CORDIC is particularly well-suited for handheld calculators, an application for which cost is much more important than speed (e.g., chip gate count has to be minimized). Also the CORDIC subroutines for trigonometric and hyperbolic functions can share most of their code.[8]

The CORDIC core implements a generalized coordinate rotational digital computer (CORDIC) algorithm, initially developed by Volder to iteratively solve trigonometric equations, and later generalized by Walther[2] to solve a broader range of equations, including the hyperbolic and square root equations. The CORDIC core implements the following equation types:

- Rectangular <-> Polar Conversion
- Trigonometric
- Hyperbolic
- Square Root

Two architectural configurations are available for the CORDIC core:

- A fully parallel configuration with single-cycle data throughput at the expense of silicon area

• A word serial implementation with multiple-cycle throughput but occupying a small silicon area

A coarse rotation is performed to rotate the input sample from the full circle into the first quadrant. (The coarse rotation stage is required as the CORDIC algorithm is only valid over the first quadrant). An inverse coarse rotation stage rotates the output sample into the correct quadrant. The CORDIC algorithm introduces a scale factor to the amplitude of the result, and the CORDIC core provides the option of automatically compensating for the CORDIC scale factor.

Features of CORDIC V4.0:

- Drop-in module for Virtex-7 and Kintex-7, Virtex-6, Virtex-5, Virtex-4, Spartan-6, Spartan-3/XA, Spartan-3A/XA/AN/3A DSP and Spartan-3E/XA FPGAs
- Functional configurations
- Vector rotation (polar to rectangular)
- Vector translation (rectangular to polar)
- Sin and Cos
- Sinh and Cosh
- Arctan and Arctanh
- Square root
- Optional coarse rotation module to extend the range of CORDIC from the first quadrant ($+Pi/4$ to $- Pi/4$ Radians) to the full circle
- Optional amplitude compensation scaling module to compensate for the CORDIC algorithm's output amplitude scale factor
- Output rounding modes: Truncation, Round to Pos Infinity, Round to Pos/Neg Infinity, and Round to Nearest Even
- Word serial architectural configuration for small area
- Parallel architectural configuration for high throughput
- Control of the internal add-sub precision
- Control of the number of add-sub iterations
- Optional input and output registers
- Optional control signals: CE, ND, SCLR, RFD, and RDY

34

- X and Y data formats: Signed Fraction, Unsigned Fraction, and Unsigned Integer
- Phase data formats: Radian, Pi Radian
- Fully synchronous design using a single clock
- For use with Xilinx CORE Generator™ and Xilinx System Generator for DSP, v13.1.

4.3 Virtex – 4 FPGA:

The Virtex series of FPGAs have integrated features that include FIFO and ECC logic, DSP blocks, PCI-Express controllers, Ethernet MAC blocks, and high-speed transceivers. In addition to FPGA logic, the Virtex series includes embedded fixed function hardware for commonly used functions such as multipliers, memories, serial transceivers and microprocessor cores. These capabilities are used in applications such as wired and wireless infrastructure equipment, advanced medical equipment, test and measurement, and defence systems. Some Virtex family members are available in radiation-hardened packages, specifically to operate in space where harmful streams of high-energy particles can play havoc with semiconductors. The Virtex-4QV FPGA was designed to be 100 times more resistant to radiation than previous radiation-resistant models and offers a ten-fold increase in performance. The XC4VSX55 Virtex-4 was used in our project.

Figure 4.10: Virtex-4 series FPGA

Combining Advanced Silicon Modular Block (ASMBL™) architecture with a wide variety of flexible features, the Virtex®-4families from Xilinx greatly enhances programmable logic design capabilities, making it a powerful alternative to ASICtechnology. Virtex-4 FPGAs comprise three platform families—LX, FX, and SX—offering multiple feature choices andcombinations to address all complex applications. The wide array of Virtex-4 FPGA hard-IP core blocks includes thePowerPC® processors (with a new APU interface), tri-mode Ethernet MACs, 622 Mb/s to 6.5 Gb/s serial transceivers,dedicated DSP slices, high-speed clock management circuitry, and source-synchronous interface blocks. The basic Virtex-4FPGA building blocks are enhancements of those found in the popular Virtex, Virtex-E, Virtex-II, Virtex-II Pro, andVirtex-II Pro X product families, so previous-generation designs are upward compatible. Virtex-4 devices are produced on astate-of-the-art 90 nm copper process using 300 mm (12-inch) wafer technology.

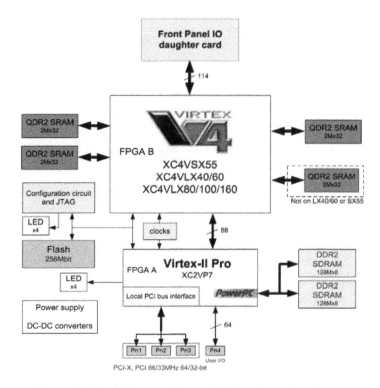

Figure 4.11: Block Diagram of Virtex 4 FPGA evaluation board

The main use of the Virtex-4 family is Unmatched Density, Highest Performance, Powerful Feature set, Best Cost structure. Virtex-4 has increased functionality when compared to the earlier series. It has the most advanced process technology: Advanced 90nm process technology, 11 layer copper metallization, has triple- oxide technology for lower quiescent power consumption. The most advanced parallel I/O interfacing capability: it has Universal connectivity – support for 26 electrical standards, ChipSync™ technology, XCITE DCI.

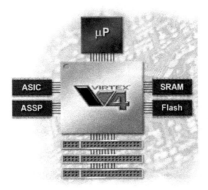

Figure 4.12: Viretx-4 I/O

The main breakthrough with ChipSync technology is the pre-engineered source synchronous logic Embedded in all I/O. The key advantages are easier design, higher performance, and resource savings. Virtex-4 has serial I/O which is very much advanced in its time. Virtex-4 RocketIO™ transceivers: Full-duplex serial transceiver blocks with integrated SERDES and Clock and Data Recovery (CDR). It operates at 622 Mbps to >10 Gbps operation.Widest Range of Operation which is Compatible with Virtex-II Pro and it supports chip-to-chip, backplane, chip-to-optics.

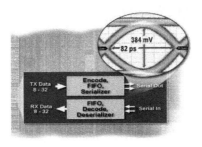

Figure 4.13: Serial I/O

Virtex-4 families have smart RAM hierarchy, it has distributed RAM/SRL 16 : very efficient, localized memory, minimal impact on logical routing , great for small FIFOs. They

38

have on chip BRAM/FIFO: efficient on-chip blocks, optional FIFO logic, ideal for midsized buffers. With fast memory interfaces: cost effective bulk storage, memory controller cores, and large memory requirements. Virtex-4 devices are user-programmable gate arrays withvarious configurable elements and embedded cores optimized for high-density and high-performance systemdesigns. Virtex-4 devices implement the following functionality:

I/O blocks provide the interface between package pins and the internal configurable logic. Most popular and leading-edge I/O standards are supported by programmable I/O blocks (IOBs). The IOBs are enhanced for source-synchronous applications. Source-synchronous optimizations include per-bit deskew, data serializer/deserializer, clock dividers, and dedicated local clocking resources.

Configurable Logic Blocks (CLBs), the basic logic elements for Xilinx FPGAs, provide combinatorial and synchronous logic as well as distributed memory and SRL16 shift register capability.

Block RAM modules provide flexible 18Kbit true dual-port RAM that arecascadable to form larger memory blocks. In addition, Virtex-4 FPGA block RAMs contain optional programmable FIFO logic for increased device utilization

The XtremeDSP slices contain a dedicated 18 x 18-bit 2'scomplement signed multiplier, adder logic, and a 48-bitaccumulator. Each multiplier or accumulator can be usedindependently. These blocks are designed to implementextremely efficient and high-speed DSP applications.

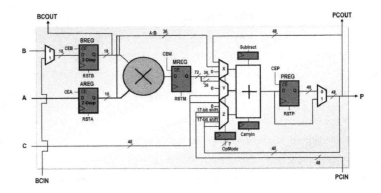

Figure 4.14: Extreme DSP in virtex-4

Digital Clock Manager (DCM) blocks provide self-calibrating, fully digital solutions for clock distribution delay compensation, clock multiplication/division, and coarse-/fine-grained clock phase shifting.The DCM and global-clock multiplexer buffers provide acomplete solution for designing high-speed clock networks.Up to twenty DCM blocks are available. To generatedeskewed internal or external clocks, each DCM can beused to eliminate clock distribution delay. The DCM alsoprovides 90°, 180°, and 270° phase-shifted versions of theoutput clocks. Fine-grained phase shifting offers higher resolution phase adjustment with fraction of the clock periodincrements. Flexible frequency synthesis provides a clockoutput frequency equal to a fractional or integer multiple ofthe input clock frequency. Virtex-4 devices have 32 global-clock MUX buffers.

Figure 4.15: DCM Clocking

Additionally, FX devices support the following embeddedsystem functionality: Integrated high-speed serial transceivers enable data rates up to 6.5 Gb/s per channel. Embedded IBM PowerPC 405 Processor RISC CPU (up to 450 MHz) with the auxiliary processor unit interface, 10/100/1000 Ethernet media-access control (EMAC) cores.

The general routing matrix (GRM) provides an array of routing switches between each component. Each programmable element is tied to a switch matrix, allowing multipleconnections to the general routing matrix. The overall programmable interconnection is hierarchical and designed tosupport high-speed designs.All programmable elements, including the routingresources, are controlled by values stored in static memorycells. These values are loaded in the memory cells duringconfiguration and can be reloaded to change the functionsof the programmable elements.[11]

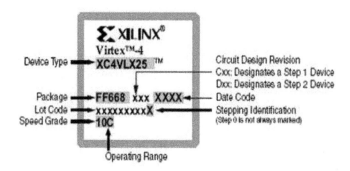

Figure 4.16: Virtex-4 Device Package Marking

Main use of Virtex-4 in defence and Government organisations is because Virtex-4 Secure Chip AES Provides Maximum Design Security. The Bitstreams encrypted with 256-bit AES algorithm. Cryptographic keys automatically erased upon malicious tampering.[11]

41

CHAPTER 5

EXPERIMENTAL WORK

5.1 Clutter Signal simulation in MATLAB:

In this project clutter signal is simulated using Gaussian distribution. Initially a uniform Random number is generated. There are mainly two methods to generate a Pseudorandom number sequence, one is Tausworthe Sequence Generation method and the other is Mixed Congruential method. This two methods have been used to simulate Pseudorandom number sequence with unit uniform distribution. Box-Muller Transformation is applied to the PRN for generating the Gaussian random variable. Each step in the simulation is explained below.

5.1.1 Generation of Pseudo Random number:

To generate any kind of noise such as Gaussian noise, Rayleigh noise, exponential noise, chi-squared noise, can be generated from unit uniform random variables. Unit uniform random variables are, in turn, generated from random number sequences. True noise, a stochastic process, can never be manufactured (or generated) by a deterministic machine such as computer. In other words, true random number sequences can never be generated by computer programs, since the true random numbers do not repeat, do not have cyclic periods, do not have an end. However, we can generate a random number sequence as close to the a random sequence as we wish with the following conditions.

The conditions are described as follows.

1.The pseudorandom number (PRN) sequence has a finite length N.

2. The PRN x, i = 1, 2, 3, . . . N, occurs only once in the total population N.

3. The PRN sequence must be contiguous in the range; that is, there shall be no missing nor duplicated number in N.

4. The sequence must not have periodicity in the range.

5.1.2 Pseudorandom Number and Unit Uniform Variables:

A random number sequence that a computer program generates that meets the conditions above is called a PRN sequence. Some commercially available programs claim to generate random numbers but fail to meet the conditions, especially condition(3),the contiguity. Among many techniques of generating PRNs, we choose the mixed congruential method. The mixed congruential method is compact, portable, and easy-to-understand. The mixed congruential method is described by [1].

$$x_{i+1} = a. \ x_i + c \quad (\text{modulo m}) \ (4.1)$$

where

a: Multiplier constant;

x_i: Initial seed;

c: Increment constant;

m:Modulus constant, the total population of the sequence N, must be a prime number. Equation (5.1).The 37 is a prime number and the total population of the pseudorandom sequence. The PRNs generated are:

9   12   27   28   33   21   35   31   11   22

3   19   25   18   20   30   6   34   26   23

8   7   2   14   37   4   24   13   32   15

10   17   19   5   29   1   9

The rules for specifying two integer constants "a" and "c" are mentioned in the footnote of the program. The rules are not very strict since any rule placed upon the randomness should not be binding. The rules should be taken as a guideline. To check the correctness of the random number sequences, PRN_MISS.CPP is written. In the program the random numbers are rank-ordered in ascending order of magnitude for a quick check on the condition (3).

1	2	3	4	5	6	7	8	9	9
10	11	12	13	14	15	16	17	18	19
20	21	22	23	24	25	26	27	28	29
30	31	32	33	34	35	37			

The duplicated number is 9, and the missing number is 36. The PRN is correctedbyreplacingoneoftheduplicatednumberswiththemissingnumber.ThecorrectedPRNsequen ceisnowcontiguous,distinctive,anduniformlydistributedintherange[1,37],withnomissingorduplicat ednumbers.

9	12	27	28	33	21	35	21	11	22
3	19	25	18	20	30	6	34	26	23
8	7	2	14	37	3	24	13	32	15
10	17	15	5	29	1	36 (5.2)			

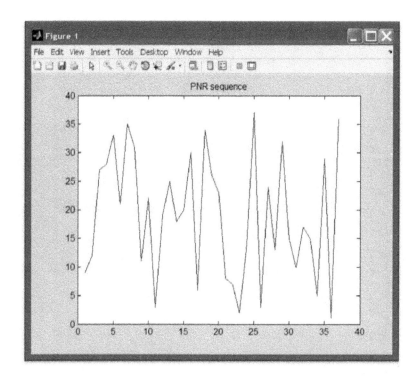

Figure 5.1: PNR Sequence of (5.2)

The mixed congruential method is versatile as well; another independent PRN sequence can be generated by changing the constant "a" and/or "c" and the initial seed x_i. A large number of independent PRN sequences would be obtained with the same population. As a demonstration we have written PRN37B.CPP by changing the increment constant "c."

7   37   2   12   25   16   8   5   27   26

21   33   19   23   6   32   14   35   29   36

34   24   11   20   28   31   9   10   15   3

17   13   30   4   22   1   18   (5.3)

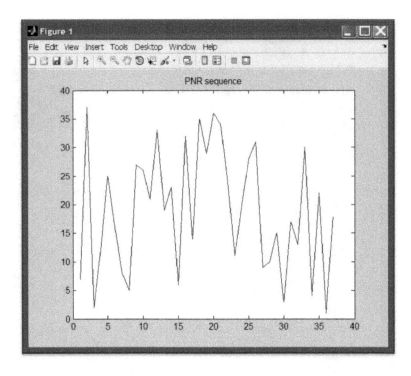

Figure 5.2:PNR Sequence of (5.1)

The unit uniform variables are obtained by simply scaling (5.2) or (5.3).

$$u_{i=}\frac{PRN_i}{N}$$

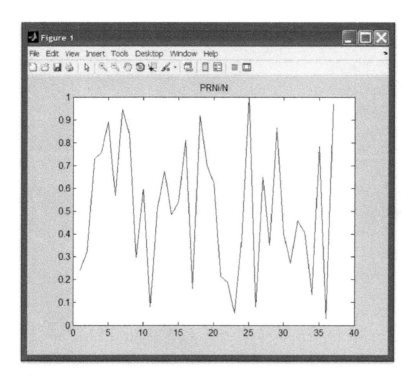

Figure 5.3: unit uniform variables are obtained by simply scaling (5.2)

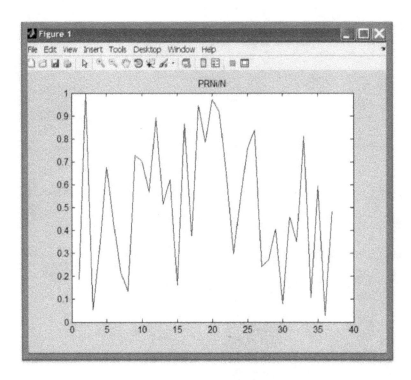

Figure 5.4: unit uniform variables are obtained by simply scaling (5.3)

The probability density function of a unit uniform random variable is shown in Figure 5.5; no missing data or duplication of data is emphasized. Unit uniform random variables are the basic building components of white Gaussian noise. White Gaussian is, in turn, the building component of all other noise.

5.1.3PRN   Generation of an Arbitrary Population:

We have employed the mixed congruential method in generating PRNs. The primary reason for selecting this method is that it is a simple algorithm, portable and versatile. Ashortcomingmaybethatitrequiresamodulooperationonaprimenumber. Theprimenumberi sthetotalpopulationofthePRNsequence.Supposewewish

48

Frequency of occurance, or probability density function

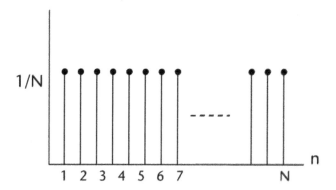

Figure 5.5 Probability density function, unit uniform random variables.

to generate random numbers different from the prime number, yet we demand acontiguity: no missing, no duplication. We follow the steps described below.[4]

1. Select a prime number m immediately larger than the desired n.

Desired Population "n"	Prime Number "m"
32	37
64	67
100	101
128	131

256	257
.	.
.	.
512	521
1024	1031
.	.
.	.

2. Generate a PRN sequence by the mixed congruential method with modulo "m" and the proper choice of "a," "c" and the initial seed.

$$x_{i+1} = a.x_i + c \quad \text{(offset by one)}$$

$$x_{i+1} = (a.x_i + c) - 1 \quad \text{(offset by zero)}$$

3. Search and find the missing numbers and pair of duplicated numbers, and correct PRN sequence.

4. Discard the highest number(s) and form the "n" random sequence that is contiguous in the range.

5.2 White Gaussian Noise:

White Gaussian noise is generated from a pair of independent unit uniform random variables $u_1(i)$ and $u_2(i)$.

$$G_{in}(i) = \sqrt{-2 log R1} . \cos 2\varPi. R2$$

$$G_{qd}(i) = \sqrt{-2 log R1} . \sin 2\varPi. R2 \quad (4.4)$$

$G_{in}(i)$ and $G_{qd}(i)$ are the in-phase and quadrature phase Gaussian noise components respectively. The "white" implies that the noise is uniform across the

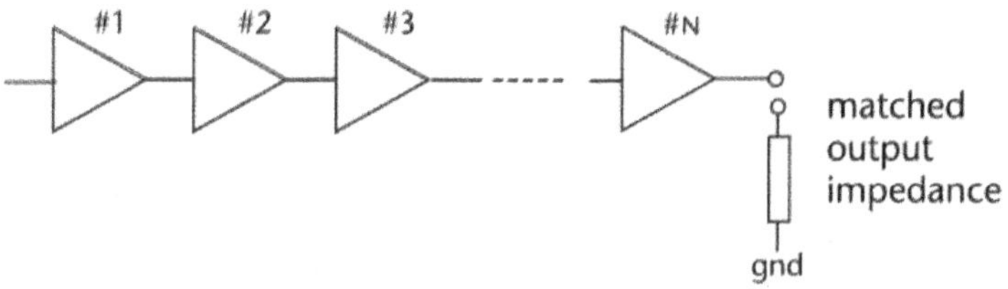

Figure 5.6:cascaded amplifiers.

frequency spectrum. "Gaussian" or sometimes "normal" refers to the amplitude distribution, the probability density function of the random variables, or the frequency of occurrence in the noise stream.

Consider the amplifier chain in Figure 5.6. The last amplifier is terminated with a matched impedance.

If we assume that the amplifiers are ideal and there is no band-limiting, the output is white Gaussian noise. When we intersperse bandpass filters between the amplifiers, the output noise is no longer white. We call the output a narrow band Gaussian noise. Consider a typical receiver chain as shown Figure 5.7. We call them the outputs I-channel and Q-channel baseband Gaussian noise, without the adjective "white."

Both of them have a semi closed range instead of a double-closed range of [0.0, 1.0]. The semi closed range is a temporary necessity for the natural logarithm involved (natural logarithm of zero is undefined).

Since the noise power of the Gaussian distribution is given by,

noise power = mean-squared + variance

51

an error in nonzero mean and an ill-conditioned variance cause an intractable confusion in analysis of a result of signal processing. They are tested so that the mean and variance are exactly 0.0 and 1.0 respectively. Gaussian random variables with a nonzero mean and a specified variance other than unity are generated by,

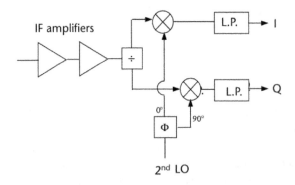

Figure 5.7 Typically receiver block diagram

G(mean, var) = mean + σ. G(0.0, 1.0)

The in-phase Gaussian noise component is shown in Figure 5.8. The probability density function in the bar graph is attached to the right. We expect the bar graph to approach to a normal when the number of samples is increased.

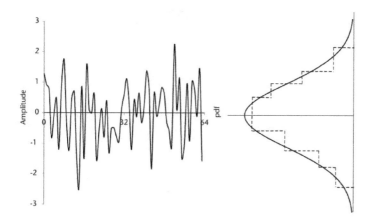

Figure 5.8 Gaussian noise, G(mean=0.0, var =1.0).

Gaussian random variables are generated by (5.4).

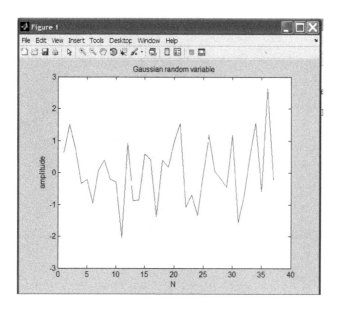

Figure 5.9 Gaussian random variable of $G_{in}(i)$.

53

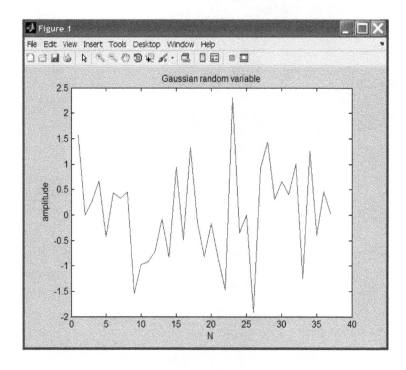

Figure 5.10 Gaussian random variable of $G_{qd}(i)$.

Gaussian distribution is given by

$$f_g(x) = \frac{1}{\sqrt{2\Pi}\sigma}\left(\frac{-(x - m)^2}{2\sigma^2}\right)$$

where,

x = Gaussian random variable $G_{in}(i)$ or $G_{qd}(i)$.

σ = standard deviation

σ^2 = variance

m = mean

54

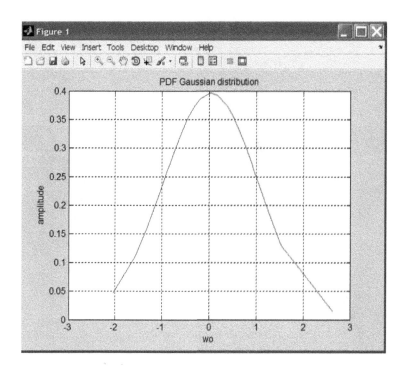

Figure 5.11 PDF of Gaussian distribution using Gaussian random variable $G_{in}(i)$.

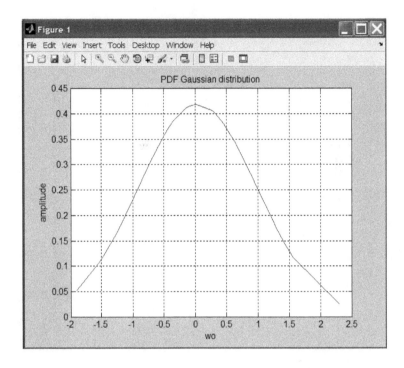

Figure 5.12: PDF of Gaussian distribution using Gaussian random Variable$G_{qd}(i)$.

5.3 Simulating the Uniform random number in Xilinx ISE:

The simulation of two Gaussian random variables$G_{in}(i)$ and $G_{qd}(i)$ as mentioned in eq(5.4), requires Pseudo random number sequence with unit uniform random variable. The implementation of uniform random variable in Xilinx as follows.

5.3.1 Simulating the Uniform random number Using Improved Tausworthe Sequence Generator Architecture:

The Linear Congruence Generator (LCG) and Feedback Shift Register (FSR) are two kinds of popular generator of uniform random number. In the ASIC design, we have employed the Tausworthe sequence generator belonging to the FSR for generating uniform random number. First, the Tausworthe sequence generator comprises registers and is easily implemented in circuit. Second, with careful selection of prime polynomial, the Tausworthe generator has

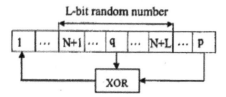

good randomness properties.

Figure 5.13 Shift register method for uniform random number generation.

The simplest way of a hardware implementation is to realize the original idea of the Tausworthe sequence as shown in Fig.5.13. Only one p-bit long shift register with **L** -bit output somewhere between the first and **pth** bit, and a two-input *XOR* element feeding the result to1 the first bit would be required. Such an architecture would be slow, because **L** clock cycles are needed to update completely the output bit position.

We present an improved architecture of the Tauthworthe generator. Using the improved architecture, the throughput can be increased to Ltimes of the conventional one, where **L** indicates the output bit length. The basic principle of the improved architecture is described as by following conditions

   Simply, let $p = Lq < p / 2$ (it has been proved that generators based on trinomial $1 + X q + X p$ exhibit good runs and uniformity properties if $p = L$, $q < p / 2$).

The algorithm for calculating the Uniform random variable for Gaussian PDF is as follows.

   step 1. Generate a random number say 'rand' using linear feedback shift register.

   Let $a1 = (a_n, ..., a_{n+p-1})$, where a1 is register with word length p of rand.

   step 2. First, let b1=a1, where b1 is also register with word length p, then, left shift the b1 by q bits and pad with zeros, we obtain $b1 = (a_{n+q},...,a_{n+p-1},0,...,0)$.where p-q bits= $a_{n+q},...,a_{n+p-1}$, q= 0,....,0.

   step 3. Let a2= a1 XOR b1 , we have a2= $(a_{n+p}, ..., a_{n+p+(p-q)-1}, a_{n+p-q},..a_{n+p-1})$.

   step 4. Let b2=a2, right shift the b2 by p-q bits and pad with zeros, we get b2= (0,0....0,a_{n+p},...,$a_{n+p+q-1}$) . where p-q bits= 0,0....0,q= a_{n+p},...,$a_{n+p+q-1}$.

step 5. Let a3= a2 XOR b2, we now have a3=(a_{n+p},...,$a_{n2+p-q-1}$,a_{n+2p-q},...,a_{n+2p-1}).

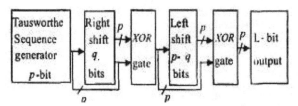

Figure 5.14 Improved Tausworthe generator architecture

Despite adding two levels of XOR elements to form a concurrent network, but a p-bit random number is generated during each shifting operation. So the throughput of the improved architecture is about as p times (p=L) as the original Tausworthe sequence generator, but the strings of consecutive bit are identical as the original ones.

Tausworthe has shown that the random number sequence yield good properties when large and carefully chosen values of p and q are used. The process of choosing good values of p and q is mapped to the trinomial $1+x^q + x^p$ where p should be chosen in such a way that 2^p-1 is a prime number, q<p/2 and q is neither too small nor too close to p/2.

e	Value	1,480 ns	1,490 ns	1,500 ns	1,510 ns	1,520 ns	1,530 ns	1,540 ns
clk	0							
random_num[7:0]	54	105	54	27	141	198	95	177
rand_12[7:0]	01011011	10110111	01011011	10101101	11010110	01101101	10111101	11011011
a1[7:0]	01011011	10110111	01011011	10101101	11010110	01101101	10111101	11011011
a2[7:0]	00110111	01101011	00110111	00011001	10001110	11000111	01100001	10110011
a3[7:0]	00110110	01101001	00110110	00011011	10001101	11000110	01100011	10110001
b1[7:0]	01101110	11011100	01101100	10110100	01011000	10101100	11011100	01101000
b2[7:0]	00000011	00000010	00000001	00000010	00000011	00000001	00000010	00000011
rand[7:0]	91	183	91	173	214	107	181	218

1,498.749 ns

Figure 5.15: Simulation of uniform random variable in Xilinx

5.4. Simulating the Gaussian random variable:

For simulating Gaussian random variable we use Coordinate Rotation Digital Computer(CORDIC) Algorithm. In this ASIC design, we have employed CORDIC algorithm for performing trigonometric operation, logarithm operation and square root operation. First, the pipelined CORDIC can satisfy the high speed and high accuracy requirement of the ASIC design. Second, the CORDIC element is illustrated in Figure 5.16

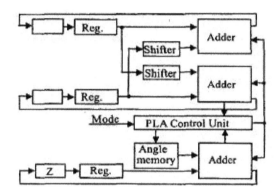

Figure.5.16 Architecture of CORDIC element

5.4.1 The circuit diagram:

The logical block diagram of RNG is illustrated in Figure 5.17.it is divided into two main parts: computation part and interface part. The computation part fulfils the required arithmetic operation for synthesis random numbers, the interface part stores the synthesised random numbers and realizes connection with the processor element outside chip.

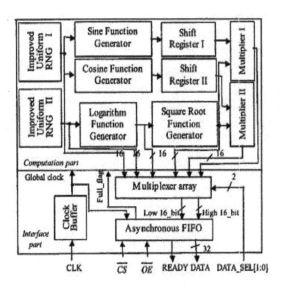

Figure 5.17 logic block diagram of RNG.

The clutter signal which follows the Gaussian PDF is simulated in Xilinx ISE. The simulation waveforms are shown in **Figure 5.18**. The signals Gaussian random variable $G_{in}(i)$ and $G_{qd}(i)$ (i.e., u_out and u_out1) is the required Gaussian distribution which follows the Gaussian PDF. The transformation for calculating the random variable is given below

$$G_{in}(i) = \sqrt{-2logR1}.\cos 2\Pi.R2$$

$$G_{qd}(i) = \sqrt{-2logR1}.\sin 2\Pi.R2$$

The algorithm for calculating the Gaussian random variable with is as follows.

1. Generate two random numbers using linear feedback shift register and calculate their product say 'rand'.
2. Calculate the values 1-rnd and 1+rnd.
3. Convert the values of 1-rnd and 1+rnd to 2QN format.

60

4. Generate a CORDIC IPcore for calculating the arctanh.

5. Assign the values 1-rnd and 1+rnd as numerator and denominator respectively to the CORDIC IPcore.

6. The output of IPcore gives the natural logarithm of square root of random number.

7. Shift output by one bit towards right for multiplication of output by 2.

8. Generate a CORDIC IPcore for calculating the square root.

9. Assign natural logarithm output as input with respect to CORDIC IPcore of square root.

10. The output gives square root of natural logarithm.

11. Generate a CORDIC IPcore for calculating the trigonometric functions.

12. Assign phase of 2ΠR as input to CORDIC IPcore of trigonometric.

13. The output gives cos2ΠR and sin2ΠR.

14. Find the product of square root of natural logarithm and trigonometric to get the final Gaussian random variable which follows PDF of Gaussian.

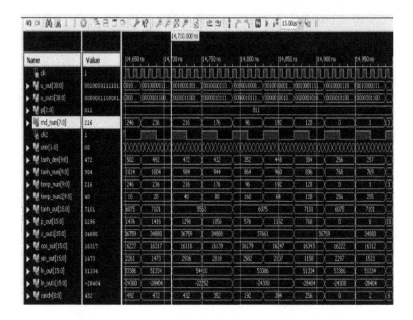

Figure 5.18: Simulating the Gaussian random variable in Xilinx

5.5 Simulating the Uniform random number in LABview:

The simulation of two Gaussian random variables $G_{in}(i)$ and $G_{qd}(i)$ as mentioned in eq(5.4), requires Pseudo random number with unit uniformrandom variable. The implementation of uniform random variable in LABveiw as follows.

5.5.1 Simulating the Pseudorandom number Using Mixed Congruential Architecture:

The Mixed congruential method is described in eq(5.1). The block diagrams of mixed congruential method logic is shown in Fig(5.19) and Fig(5.20).

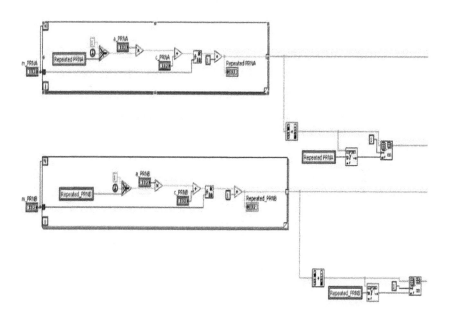

Figure 5.19: Block diagram of mixed congruential method logic part 1

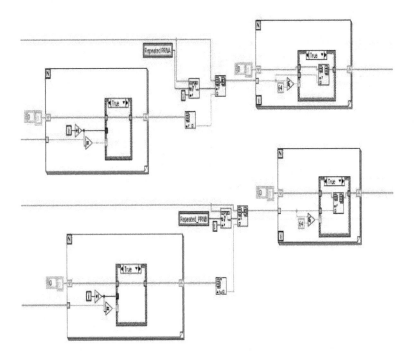

Figure 5.20: Block diagram of mixed congruential method logic part 2

5.5.2 Simulation of Gauusian random varible using Box-Muller Transformation :

The Pseudo random number sequence is converted to Guassian random variable using Box-Muller transformation.The block diagram of Box-Muller transformation logic is shown below in Fig(5.21) and Fig(5.22).

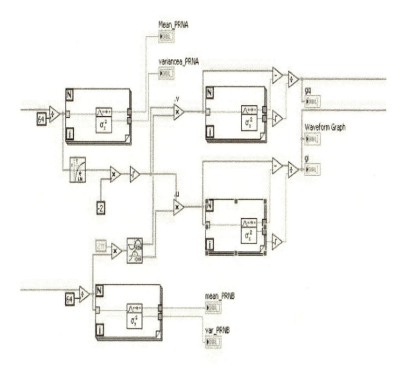

Figure 5.21: Block diagram of Box-Muller transform logic part 1.

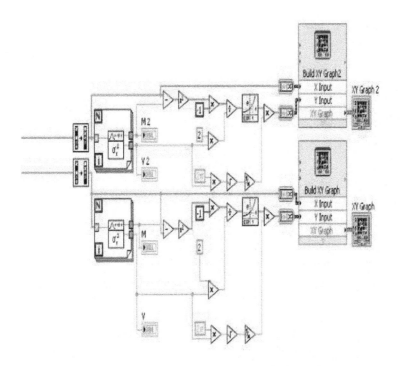

Figure 5.22: Block diagram of Box-Muller transform logic part 2.

The algorithm for simulating of Gaussian PDF is as follows.

1. Initially Pseudo random number sequence of (PRNA and PRNB) is gernerated using mixed congruential method.

2. This Pseudo random number is converted to unit uniform distribution by sorting.

3. By using Box-Muller transformation as mentioned in eq(5.4) is applied to pseudorandom number sequence with unit uniform distribution for generating the gaussian random variables(u and v).

4. By calculating mean,variance of Gaussian random variable and using Gaussion distribution,we simulate PDF of Gaussian noise.

5. Simulation result of PDF of gauissan noise is shown in Fig(5.23).

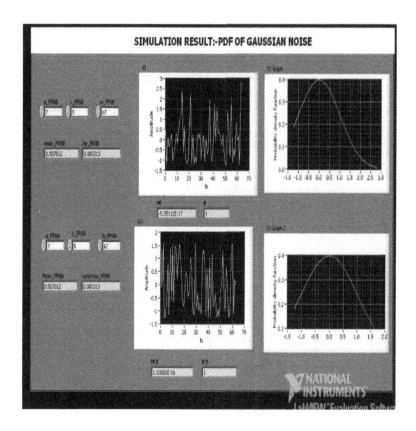

Figure 5.23: Simulation result of PDF of Gaussian noise.

5.6. Matched Filter Design:

Since the matched filter is a linear time invariant system, its output can be described mathematically by the convolution between its input and its impulse response,

$$y(t) = s(t) \bullet h(t)$$

...............................(5.1)

67

where $s(t)$ is the input signal, $h(t)$ is the matched filter impulse response(replica), and the • operator symbolically represents convolution. From the Fourier transform properties,

$$FFT\{s(t) \bullet h(t)\} = S(f) \cdot H(f)$$

.........................(5.2)

And when both signals are sampled properly, the compressed signal $y(t)$ can be computed from

$$y = FFT^{-1}\{S \cdot H\}$$

....(5.3)

where FFT^{-1} is the inverse FFT.

Figure 5.24 shows the computing the matched filter output using FFT

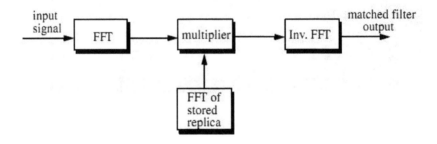

Figure 5.24: Computation of Matched filter output using FFT.

5.7. DESIGN OF CLUTTER GENERATOR:

In my honours project I have designed clutter generator in LABVIEW software.

The following steps are followed for the designing of clutter generator:

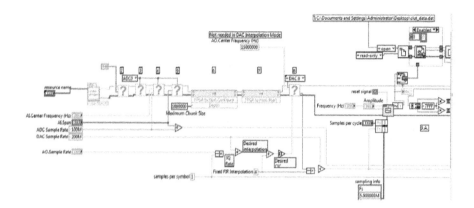

Figure.5.25: Part-1 of clutter generator LABVIEW coding

Figure.5.25 shows the 8 steps in designing clutter generator.

1. Opens a reference to the FPGA VI on the NI-5640R
2. Configure the NI-5640R Timebase to run the ADCs at 100 MH, the DACs at 200 MHz and the RTSI Clk at 50 MHz.
3. Configure ADC0 to its default settings.
4. Configure the input center frequency.
5. Configure the input decimation factor.
6. Configure size of the host side DMA buffer depth.
7. . Start the DMA buffer so data has a place to go as soon as the acquisition starts.

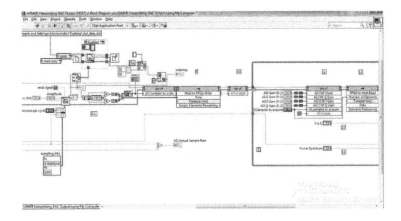

Figure.5.26: Part-2 of clutter generator LABVIEW coding

Figure 5.26 shows the following steps in designing Clutter generator.

8. Configure the output interpolation. In Interpolating DAC mode, the Center Frequency does not apply and is ignored.

9. A. In interpolating DAC mode, Real waveform samples (instead of complex IQ samples) must be downloaded to the FPGA. Due to the method that the NI 5640R transfers data to the DAC,the waveform must be decimated, converted to I16, and then combined to U32. Each U32 data type will contain sample(X) and sample(X+1).

9.B. Write the waveform to the DMA buffer so it's transfered to the FPGA.

10. Initiate the generation.

11. Set I & Q Gain for input and outupt. Also set the number of samples to acquire and start the acqusition.

12. Read from the DMA buffer the specified number of samples.

13. Plot I vs. Q.

14. Convert to floating point and plot power spectrum.

15. Verify no acquisition overflow or generation underflow has occurred.

16. Check temperature of NI-5640R and shutdown in case of errors.

70

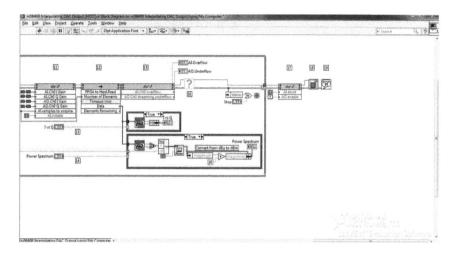

Figure.5.27: Part-3 of clutter generator LABVIEW coding

Figure.5.27 desribes the remaining steps in Clutter Generation.

17. Stop the analog acquisition and the generation
18. Reset the FPGA VI and close the reference.
19. Check for any errors and display to the user.

CHAPTER-6

PROJECT WORKING AND OUTPUT

6.1 WORKING:

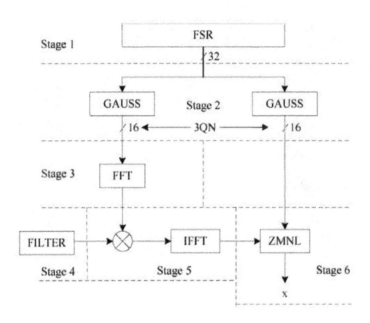

Figure 6.1: System block diagram of Lognormal Distributed Clutter Generation

The Lognormal distributed clutter generation system based on FPGA includes the random number generator, Gaussian sequence generator, fast Fourier and inverse-Fourier transformation, frequency filter and zero memory nonlinearity amplitude transformation. The system block diagram is showed in figure 6.1.

The main function of the system is described. Firstly, the random number is generated by using Feedback Shift Register (FSR); then the generated random number is used to generate the Gaussian random sequence. Stage three to stage five is the frequency filter component and this architecture is designed according to the temporal correlated characteristic of the clutter; then, the final output is generated by passing the processed data and the Gaussian random sequence through the zero memory nonlinearity amplitude transformation.[19]

6.2 Generation of random number using LFSR:

Linear Feedback Shift Register (LFSR) is used to generate a random number. A linear feedback shift register (LFSR) is ashift register whose input bit is a linear function of its previous state.The most commonly used linear function of single bits is XOR. Thus, an LFSR is most often a shift register whose input bit is driven by the exclusive-or (XOR) of some bits of the overall shift register value.Any long LFSR counter generates a long pseudo-random sequence of zeros and ones. The sequence is not exactly random since it repeats eventually, and it also follows a mathematically predictable sequence. But for most practical purposes it can be considered random.A 63-bit LFSR counter has a repetition time of (263-1) clock periods. Running at 50 MHz, such a counter repeats after more than five thousand years (5,849 years to be more precise), which is long enough to be irrelevant for most practical purposes.Based on the LFSR length different XNOR feedback taps are required to generate a maximum-length random numbers.

The XNOR feedback tap points to some LFSR are shown in **Table 6.1.**

Table 6.1: XNOR feedback tap points for LFSR

No.of bits in LFSR	Bit positions for XNOR tap points
3	3,2
4	4,3
5	5,3
6	6,5
7	7,6
8	8,6,5,4
9	9,5
10	10,7
16	16,15,13,4
32	32,22,12,1
64	64,63,61,60
128	128,126,101,99

A 10 bit LFSR with tap points at 10th and 7th bit is shown in **Figure 6.2**.

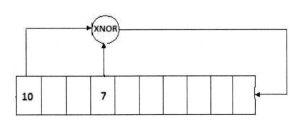

Figure 6.2: XNOR Tap points for 10 bit LFSR

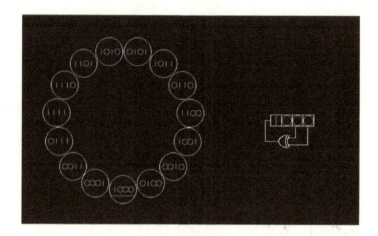

Figure 6.3: LFSR Generation

6.3 Calculating Natural Logarithm of a Number:

Xilinx provides library functions to calculate natural logarithm of a number in VHDL. But these function can be used only for simulation, they are not synthesizable. So to calculate the natural logarithm of a number the CORDIC IPcore is used. The natural logarithm of a number 'a' can be calculated using the following formula.

$$\ln(a) = 2 \tanh^{-1}\left(\frac{1-a}{1+a}\right)$$

The arctanh is computed using the CORDIC IPcore.

Steps involved in generation of Pseudo Random numbers using FPGA is shown in Figure 6.3.

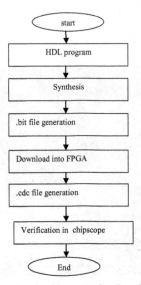

Figure 6.4: Steps involved in generating Pseudo random numbers using FPGA

HDL code is generated, simulated and synthesized using VHDL. Then .Bit file is generated .It is dumped into FPGA. By adding .cdc file, code code is verified using Chipscope Pro.

Chipscope Pro output of generating Pseudo random numbers is shown in Figure 6.5[19][21]

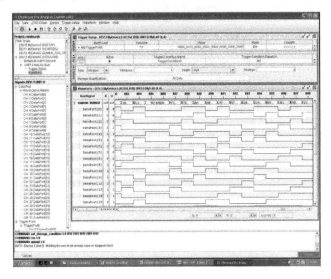

Figure 6.5: Chipscope Pro output for PRNG generation

76

6.4 Generation of Gaussian Noise:

From figure 6.1 stage-2 is generating Gaussian variable using generated PRNG.

Gaussian noise generator is designed using LABVIEW software.

Figure 6.6 shows the steps involved in generating Gaussian noise using Box-Muller technique.

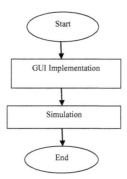

Figure 6.6: Steps involved in generating Gaussian noise in LABVEW

In the similar manner of generating PRNG GUI is implemented based on Box-Muller technique and simulated.

Figure 6.7 shows the Generated Gaussian Noise.[20]

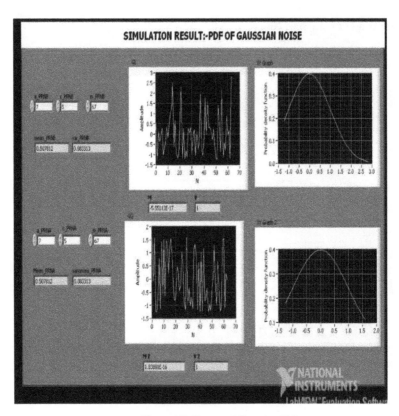

Figure 6.7: Generated Gaussian Noise

6.5. Output of Designed Matched filter:

From figure 6.1 stage -3 to stage -5 are the components of Matched filter. In this section exho signal from radar is passed through a filter and multiplied with the FFT component of Gaussian noise Inverse Fast Fourier transform is applied on the output of multiplier. The whole output is Matched filter output. Figure 6.8, Figure 6.9, Figure 6.10 shows the uncompressed echo signal,

Compressed echo signal, Matched filter time and frequency domain responses.[22]

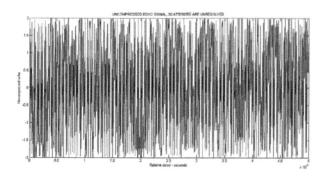

Figure 6.8: uncompressed echo signal

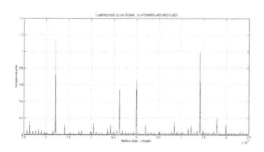

Figure 6.9: compressed echo signal

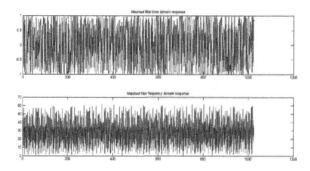

Figure 6.10: Matched filter time and frequency domain responses

79

6.6. Output of Clutter Generator:

In figure 6.1 stage-6 is output ie. Lognormal Distributed Clutter. It generated by Zero Memory Nonlinearity amplitude Transformation (ZMNL) technique.

The scheme for the generation of the Lognormal distributed clutter by ZMNL method is showed in figure 6.11.

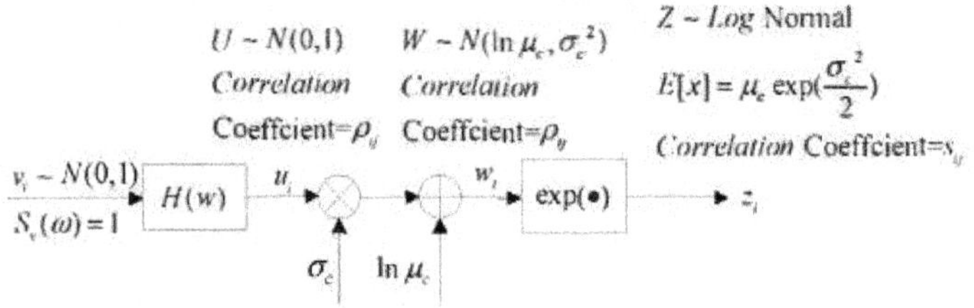

Figure 6.11: The scheme of generation of Lognormal distributed clutter by ZMNL technique

Where ρ_{ij} and s_{ij} represent the correlation coefficient of the input and output of the system and the relationship between them is as follow:

$$s_{ij} = \frac{e^{\sigma_c^2 \rho_{ij}} - 1}{e^{\sigma_c^2} - 1}$$ .... (6.1)

$$\rho_{ij} = \frac{\ln[1 + s_{ij}(e^{\sigma_c^2} - 1)]}{\sigma_c^2}$$ .... (6.2)

The output of the clutter generator is shown in figure 6.12.

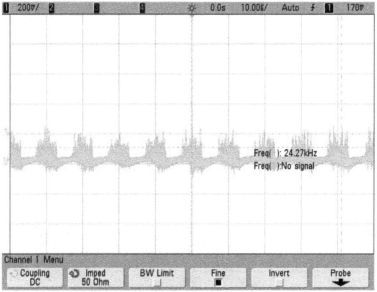

THU JUN 27 15:28:59 2013

Freq( ): 24.27kHz
Freq( ):No signal

Figure 6.12 : Generated clutter

Different samples are taken and plotted in MATLAB it gave the distribution of Lognormal distribution. The plot is shown in Figure 6.13[24]

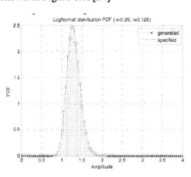

Figure 6.13: plot of taken various samples

CHAPTER 7

CONCLUSION & FUTURE SCOPE

7.1 Conclusion:

In this project is clutter is generated by using pseudo random numbers. Random numbers are generated by FPGA. Using these random numbers Gaussian noise is generated and it is simulated in LABVIEW. Matched filter is designed and the working of matched filter is simulated in MATLAB. ZMNL process is applied for the output of matched filter and Gaussian noise to convert Gaussian into non Gaussian properties. The out output is required Clutter. Range and velocity simulation is done using LABVIEW software. It is shown in Figure 7.1

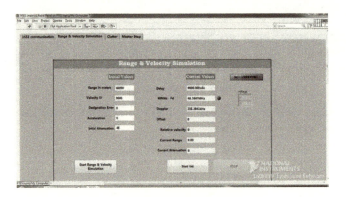

Figure 7.1: Range and Velocity simulation

7.2 Future Scope:

The Clutter implemented in FPGA can be used in radar testing and performance evaluation of RADARs. Clutter can also be used in range and velocity simulation also.

References

1. Introduction to RADAR Systems – Merrill I. Skolnik

2. Radar System analuysis – W. Kang.

3. Radar Systems Analysis and Design Using MatLab - MahafzaBassem R

4. Generating Swerling Random Sequences – Mark A. Richards

5. Design of Multilevel Radar Target Simulator – Meena D, Taniza Roy, LGM Prakasam.

6. A Guide to MATLAB – Brain R. Hunt, Ronal L.Lipsman, Jonathan M.Rosenberg.

7. Introduction to MATLAB – David Houcque

8. VHDL Programming by Example – Douglas L. Perry.

9. http://www.radartutorial.eu/

10. http://aess.cs.unh.edu/radar%20se%20List%20of%20Lectures%20.html

11. http://www.xilinx.com/support/

12. http://vhdlguru.blogspot.in

13. http://esd.cs.ucr.edu/labs/tutorial/

14. http://www.seas.upenn.edu/~ese171/vhdl/vhdl_primer.html

15. http://www.xilinx.com/support/documentation/sw_manuals/xilinx11/ise_c_using_coregen_ip.htm

16. http://www.markharvey.info/vhdl/

17. http://www.swarthmore.edu/NatSci/echeeve1/Ref/BinaryMath/NumSys.html#signfrac

18. http://www.csee.umbc.edu/portal/help/VHDL/

19. **Thottempudi Pardhu** , Usha Rani Neelakuditi ,P.Suresh **"NOVEL RANDOM SEQUENCE GENERATION AND VALIDATION USING FPGA"** in the proceedings of *International conference on Communications Networking And Signal Processing (ICCNASP-2013)* pp:295-298

20. **Thottempudi Pardhu,** Usharani Neelakuditi, Suresh Pampana **"GENERATION AND VALIDATION OF GAUSSIAN NOISE USING GAUSSIAN SEQUENCE"** in the proceedings of *IEEE International Conference on Electronics and Communications Systems 2014(ICECS2014)* pp:271-275. **(Reflecting in Scopus)**

21. **Thottempudi Pardhu,** Thottempudi Nagateja, K.N.Bhushan, N.Usha Rani **"GENERATION OF CRYPTOGRAPHICALLY SECURED PSEUDO RANDOM NUMBERS USING FPGA"** in *International Journal of Electronics And Communication Engineering And Technology (IJECET)* .V-5,Issue-2,Feb-2014,pp:21-29

83

22. **Thottempudi Pardhu** , Usha Rani Neelakuditi ,P.Suresh **"NOVEL CHARACTARIZATION AND GENERATION OF RADAR VOLUME CLUTTER USING FPGA"** in *International Journal of Applied Engineering Research (IJAER)* V-9,Issue-21,Sep-2014,pp:8523-8532 **(Reflecting in Scopus)**

23. **Thottempudi Pardhu** , A.Kavya Sree ,K.Tanuja **"DESIGN OF MATCHED FILTER FOR RADAR APPLICATIONS"** in *Elecrical And Electronics Engineering: An International Journal (ELELIJ)* V-3,Issue-4,Nov-2014,pp:1-11

24. **Thottempudi Pardhu**, N.Alekhya Reddy **"FPGA DESIGN OF CLUTTER GENERATOR FOR RADAR TESTING"** in *Circuits And Systems: An International Journal (CSIJ)* V-2, Issue-1, Jan-2015, PP:13-24

APPENDIX

A. Source codes for the implementation of project:

A.1. VHDL code for generation of Pseudo Random Numbers:

```
library IEEE;

use IEEE.STD_LOGIC_1164.ALL;

use IEEE.STD_LOGIC_ARITH.ALL;

use IEEE.STD_LOGIC_UNSIGNED.ALL;

library UNISIM;

use UNISIM.VComponents.all;

entity RANDM is

  Port ( random_num : out  STD_LOGIC_VECTOR (31 downto 0);

       clk_out:out  STD_LOGIC;

       CLK : in  STD_LOGIC);

end RANDM;

architecture Behavioral of RANDM is

begin

OBUF_inst : OBUF

  generic map (

    DRIVE => 12,

    IOSTANDARD => "DEFAULT",

    SLEW => "SLOW")

  port map (

  O => clk_out,

  I => clk

  );
```

```
process(clk)
variable rand_temp : std_logic_vector(31 downto 0):=(31 => '1',others => '0');
variable temp : std_logic := '0';
begin
if(rising_edge(clk)) then
temp := rand_temp(31) xor rand_temp(30);
rand_temp(31 downto 1) := rand_temp(30 downto 0);
rand_temp(0) := temp;
end if;
random_num <= rand_temp;
end process;
end Behavioral;
```

A.2. MATLAB code for generating Random numbers using Box-Muller technique:

```
function qGaussian = qGaussianDist(nSamples,qDist)

% Returns random deviates drawn from a q-gaussian distribution
% The number of samples returned is nSamples.
% The q that characterizes the q-Gaussian is given by qDist
%
% Check that q < 3
if 0 < 3

    % Calaulate the q to be used on the q-log
    qGen = (1 + 0)/(3 - 0);
```

```matlab
    % Initialize the output vector
    qGaussian = zeros(1,1000);
        % Loop through and populate the output vector
    for k = 1:1000

        % Get two uniform random deviates
        % from built-in rand function
        u1 = rand;
        u2 = rand;

        % Apply the generalized Box-Muller algorithm,
        % taking only one of two possible values
        qGaussian(k) = sqrt(2*log_q(u1,qGen))*sin(2*pi*u2);

    end

% Return 0 and give a warning if q >= 3
else

    warning('The input q value must be less than 3')
    qGaussian = 0;

end

end

function a = log_q(x,q)
%
% Returns the q-log of x, using q
% Check to see if q = 1 (to double precision)
    if abs(q - 1) < 10*eps
```

87

```matlab
        % If q is 1, use the usual natural logarithm
        a = log(x);

    else

        % If q differs from 1, use the definition of the q-log
        a = (x.^(1-q) - 1)./(1-q);

    end

end
```

A.3. MATLAB code for generation of Gaussian noise:

```matlab
% estimation of gaussian density and distribution functions
clc;
clear all;
close all;
% defining the range for random variable
dx=0.01;
x=-3:dx:3;
[m,n]=size(x);
% defining the paameters of pdf
mu_x=1;
sig_x=0.5;
% computing the pdf
px1=[];
a=1/(sqrt(2*pi)*sig_x);
for j=1:n
```

```
    px1(j)=a*exp([-((x(j)-mu_x)/sig_x)^2]/2);
end
% computing cumulative distribution function
cum_px(1)=0;
for j=2:n
    cum_px(j)=cum_px(j-1)+dx*px1(j);
end
% plotting the results
figure(1)
plot(x,px1);grid
axis([-3 3 0 1]);
title(['Gaussian pdf for mu_x=0 and sigma_x=',num2str(sig_x)]);
xlabel('-->x')
ylabel('-->pdf')
figure(2)
plot(x,cum_px);grid
axis([-3 3 0 1]);
title(['Gaussian probability density function for mu_x=0 and sigma_x=',num2str(sig_x)]);
title('\ite^{omega\tau}=cos(\omega\tau)+isin(\omega\tau)')
xlabel('-->x')
ylabel('-->pdf')
```

A.4. MATLAB code for design of matched filter:

```
function [y] = matched_filter(nscat, taup, f0, b, rmin, rrec, scat_range, scat_rcs, winid)
%
eps = 1.0e-16;
htau = 0.005 / 2.;
c = 3.e8;
n = fix(2. * 0.005 * 16000000);
```

```
m = 10;
nfft = 2.^m;
x(2,1:nfft) = 0;
y(1:nfft) = 0;
replica(1:nfft) = 0.;
if( 2 == 0.)
  win(1:nfft) = 1.;
  win =win';
else
  if(2 == 1.)
    win = hamming(nfft);
  else
    if( 2 == 2.)
      win = kaiser(nfft,pi);
    else
      if(2 == 3.)
        win = chebwin(nfft,60);
      end
    end
  end
end
deltar = c / 2. / 16000000;
max_rrec = deltar * nfft / 2.;
maxr = max(150.05) - 150;
if(200 > max_rrec | maxr >= 200 )
  'Error. Receive window is too large; or scatterers fall outside window'
  Return
end
trec = 2. * 200 / c;
deltat = 0.005 / nfft;
t = 0: deltat:0.005-eps;
```

```
uplimit = max(size(t));
replica(1:uplimit) = exp(i * 2.* pi * (.5 * (16000000/0.005) .* t.^2))
figure(3)
subplot(2,1,1)
plot(real(replica))
title('Matched filter time domain response')
subplot(2,1,2)
plot(fftshift(abs(fft(replica))));
title('Matched filter frequency domain response')
for j = 1:1:2
  t_tgt = 2. * (150.05 - 150) / c +htau;
  x(j,1:uplimit) = 1 .* exp(i *  2.* pi * (.5 * (16000000/0.005) .* (t+t_tgt).^2));
  y = y + x(j,:);
end
figure(1)
plot(t,real(y),'k')
xlabel ('Relative delay - seconds')
ylabel ('Uncompressed echo')
title ('UNCOMPRESSED ECHO SIGNAL, SCATTERERS ARE UNRESOLVED ')
rfft = fft(replica,nfft);
yfft = fft(y,nfft);
out= abs(ifft((rfft .* conj(yfft)) .* win' )) ./ (nfft);
figure(2)
time = -htau:deltat:htau-eps;
plot(time,out,'k')
xlabel ('Relative delay - seconds')
ylabel ('Compressed echo')
title ('COMPRESSED ECHO SIGNAL ,SCATTERERS ARE RESOLVED')
grid
```

A.5. VHDL code for generation of Pulse Repetition Frequency (PRF) signal:

```
library IEEE;

use IEEE.STD_LOGIC_1164.ALL;

use IEEE.STD_LOGIC_ARITH.ALL;

use IEEE.STD_LOGIC_UNSIGNED.ALL;

entity delay_sig4 is

    Port ( clk,en1,prf_new : in  STD_LOGIC;

        initialdelay_clk1 : in  STD_LOGIC_VECTOR (15 downto 0);

        delay_clutter : in  STD_LOGIC_VECTOR (15 downto 0);

        PRF_DELAY : out  STD_LOGIC;

        PRF_CLUTTER : out  STD_LOGIC);

end delay_sig4;

architecture Behavioral of delay_sig4 is

        signal prf_delay1, prf_clutter1 : std_logic;

        type shiftregister is array  (20000 downto 0 ) of std_logic;

        signal shift_prf:shiftregister:=(others=>'0');

begin

PRF_DELAY<=(not(PRF_DELAY1));

PRF_CLUTTER  <=(not(prf_clutter1));
```

```vhdl
prf_clutter1 <= shift_prf(conv_integer(delay_clutter));

prf_delay1 <= shift_prf(conv_integer(initialdelay_clk1));

process(clk)

begin

        if(clk'event and clk='1')then

        if en1='1' then

                shift_prf <= shift_prf(19999 downto 0) & prf_new;

        end if;

        end if;

end process;

end Behavioral;
```

B.ANALYZING THE DESIGN USING CHIPSCOPE:

1. Right click on the top module of the design intended for verification or debugging, and select new source. Then select **ChipScope Definition and Connection File** as shown in Figure b.1.

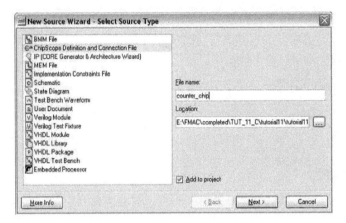

Figure b.1: Chipscope module section.

2. Then give an appropriate name for the **file name**. Press **next** and select the **hierarchy level** at Which the analysis is intended to be performed and then press **next** and then do **finish**.

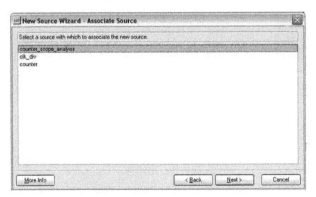

Figure b.2: Hirarchy section.

94

3. The first two steps will cause a new file (with file name as given) to be created in the source

Window under the project hierarchy as shown in Figure b.3.

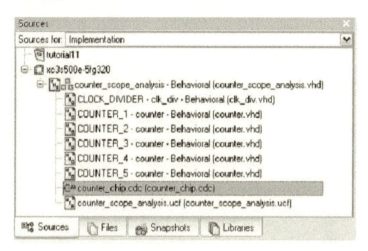

Figure b.3: Chipscope Module Location

4. Double click on this new source file which cause the below window to pop up. Keep the default settings with **Use SRLs** and **Use RPMs** as checked.

This will enable the tool to use Shift Register LUTs instead of flip flops and multiplexers thereby effectively reducing the size and improving the performance of the core generator. RPMs contain RLOC constraints which define the order and structure of the underlying design primitives. Use of RPMs will enable the tool to use relationally placed macros (like FMAP, HMAP, ROM, RAM, etc) allowing logic blocks to be placed relative to increase speed and use die resources efficiently substituting hard macros with an equivalent that can be simulated directly which again increases the core performance.

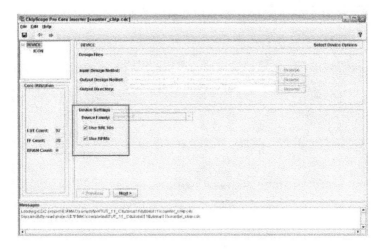

Figure b.4: SRL and RPMs

5. Press next and again leave the default conditions i.e., keep the **Disable JTAG Clock BUFG Insertion** box unchecked.

Disabling JTAG clock will cause the implementation tool to route the JTAG clock using normal routing resources instead of global clock routing resources. This might affect the high speed clock signals. So, unless the global resources are very scarce, it should not be disabled. But, disabling might introduce skew.

Figure b.5: Global clocks

6. Press **next** and then select the number of **trigger ports** and their respective **widths** depending on the design requirement.

Triggers are those signals which initiate or trigger a certain sequence of actions influencing certain signals under consideration.

Here, signal FREQUENCY is the only trigger taken into consideration (which is three bits wide) to control the counter output. Therefore, number trigger ports is set to 1 and the width is set to 3.

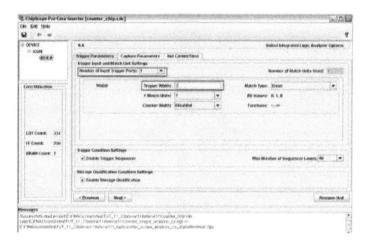

Figure b.6: Trigger options

7. Now **Match Type** should be selected. This defines the type of trigger one wants. For example: **Basic** mode, triggers depending on the specific value to which trigger is set. **Range** mode, triggers depending on the range of values in which the trigger is defined. **Extended** mode triggers depending on one or more occurrences of exact or range of trigger values to which trigger is set. A combinatorial logic (like AND/OR) or conditional logic (IF/THEN) between 2 or more signals can also be implemented into a trigger signal. Since FREQUENCY signal has definite values, Basic mode can be chosen for the Match Type in the present case.

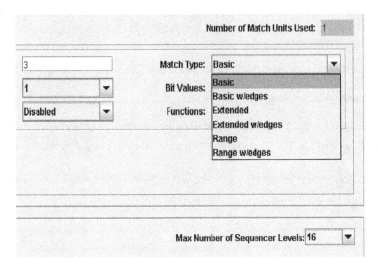

Figure b.7: Match type

8. Now uncheck or check the **Trigger Conditions Settings** i.e., **Enable Trigger Sequencer** and **Enable Storage Qualification** depending on the design requirements.

Enable Trigger Sequencer can be used to enable a 16 level trigger sequencer which aids in configuring a multi level state machine to trigger upon a user defined traversal scheme of match units.

Enable Storage Qualification can be used to filter data that is captured based on the user defined conditions that can be combined with trigger events. As the present trigger (FREQUENCY signal) is a simple and straight forward trigger, so both the boxes can be unchecked which saves little amount of logic space on the FPGA as shown in Figure b.8 (**LUT and FF count**).

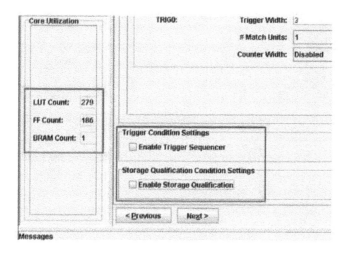

Figure b.8: Trigger and Storage Settings

9. Press **next** and depending on the design requirement uncheck or check the **Data Same As**

Trigger option.

If data is not same as trigger then define the **Data Width**.

The **Data Depth** is defined depending again on the requirements. It is recommended to put maximum limit as it can be adjusted during the analysis phase.

Select the **Rising** or **Falling** edge of the clock signal depending on whichever edge desired to sample the data.

As in the present design, the output data (Q) and trigger (FREQUENCY) are different the **Data Same As Trigger** icon is unchecked. Since the width of counter is 4-bit, data width is selected as 4. Rising edge is selected for clock edge for sampling data.

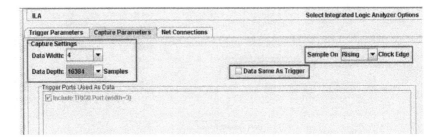

Figure b.9: Data Options

10. Press **next** and then press **Modify Connections**.

Figure b.10: Net Connections

11. Once **Modify Connections** is clicked, the below shown window will pop up. Select the

Appropriate signals from the list of nets and make connections to the respective clock, trigger

And data signals.

Once all the connections are made press **OK**.

Then press **Return to Project Navigator** and **Save Project changes**.

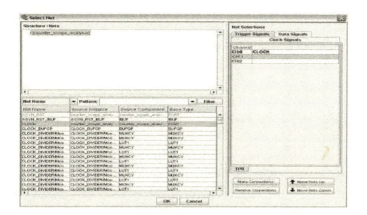

Figure b.11: Net Selections

12. Now re-implement the design using the **Implement Design** icon and then do the configuration using the **Configure Target** Device icon.

Once these steps are done successfully one is ready to analyze the design using the **Analyze Design Using ChipScope** icon (present along with the implement design and configure design icons in the processes window of the ISE tool). By double clicking this icon the following window will pop up.

Figure b.12: ChipScope Analyzer

In the top left hand corner there is an icon which is used to open the JTAG chain, click on this icon and the following window pops up. It shows all the devices it has found in the JTAG chain, press **OK.**

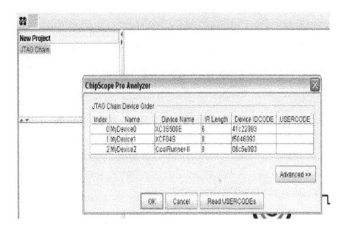

Figure b.13: JTAG chain

13. Once the list is accepted by pressing **OK** the following window shows up. Set the trigger to design criteria, adjust the data depth to the amount needed and then hit the play button (all of them are marked in red boxes). One can observe all the output signal variations and do the verification as needed.

102

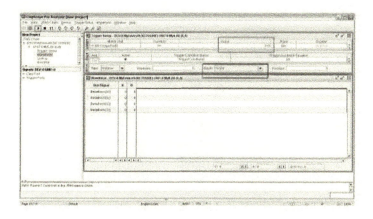

Figure b.14: Trigger and data setup

14. The data waveform for the sample counter when trigger is set to "000" is as shown in Figure b.15.

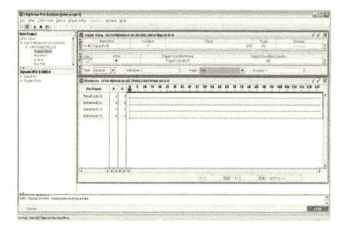

Figure b.15: Waveforms

15. Sometimes using the bus plot will be very beneficial to observe certain output signals. This can be done by selecting all the data ports and tying them into a single bus as shown in Figure b.16.

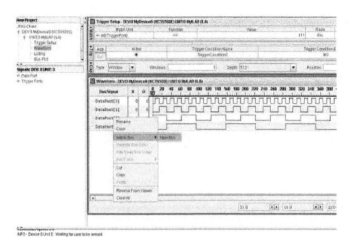

Figure b.16: Bus port creation

16. The bus plot can be viewed by clicking on the bus plot icon as shown in Figure b.17 and selecting the appropriate bus signal intended for viewing.

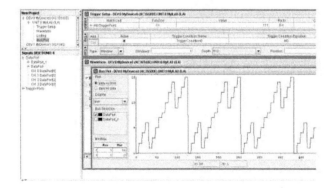

Figure b.17: Bus Plot

17. This is the signal that is directly being tapped from the FPGA on the board unlike the ISE Simulator signals which are behavioral simulated (can be observed using the test bench provided along with the sample project). So one gets to observe how the actual signal is behaving on the board which is very essential to resolve timing issues in high speed designs.

Merits and Demerits:

1. The major advantages of ChipScope compared to external logic analyzers are:

• Reduces the probe delays in analyzing the signals.

• Reduces the circuit performance degradation caused due to probing.

• Portable and convenient to analyze circuitry on FPGA.

• Cost – logic analyzers can cost over $50,000.

2. There are few limitations of ChipScope as compared to external logic analyzers which are:

• Availability of resources on the FPGA (which comes into picture for large complex designs).

• Sampling rate cannot be faster than the design clock frequency (making glitch detection not possible).

www.ingramcontent.com/pod-product-compliance
Lightning Source LLC
LaVergne TN
LVHW042338060326
832902LV00006B/244